REGINALD C. STUART is a member of the Department of History at the University of Prince Edward Island.

By the middle of the eighteenth century war had come to be regarded as a limited instrument of state policy and one that should be controlled in the interests of social justice and human progress. Thomas Jefferson's attitude towards war emerged from this Enlightenment tradition and evolved in response to the issues he faced during his career. Drawing on comments scattered through his letters and other writings and an interpretation of the policies he actually pursued, this book traces the development of Jefferson's view of war, from the time of his participation in the Continental Congress, through his years as negotiator and diplomat in Paris following the peace with Britain and independence, his terms as secretary of state, vice-president, and president during an era of European war and near war that threatened United States interests, and his years of retirement when the United States engaged in war and promulgated the Monroe Doctrine.

While Jefferson displayed an overwhelming desire to avoid war, he did not suppose that it could be eliminated. He considered it a part of nature, occasionally both just and necessary. He emphasized defence and deterrence, but he did not hesitate to use or threaten war to preserve national integrity and promote national interests during his presidency. Politically and philosophically, he was a pragmatist rather than a pacifist, ready to engage in limited war for limited objectives and as a last resort, but opposed to war as a crusade.

Throughout, Stuart's analysis of Jefferson's thinking on matters military shows a sensitive awareness of the tensions in western thought which arose in the transition from the ideas of the Enlightenment to those of the modern era.

REGINALD C. STUART

The Half-way Pacifist:
Thomas Jefferson's View of War

UNIVERSITY OF TORONTO PRESS
Toronto   Buffalo   London

© University of Toronto Press 1978
Toronto   Buffalo   London
Printed in Canada

Library of Congress Cataloging in Publication Data

Stuart, Reginald C.
The half-way pacifist.

Bibliography: p.
Includes index.
1. Jefferson, Thomas, Pres. U. S., 1743 – 1826 –
Views on war. 2. War. I. Title.
E332.2.S87   327   78 – 8232
ISBN 0-8020-5431-5

For Penni and Jonathan

Contents

'War is the father of all things.' HERACLITUS

'Wars are undertaken in order that we may live in peace without suffering wrong.' CICERO

'A necessary war is a just war.' MACHIAVELLI

'War never leaves where it found a nation.' BURKE

Preface

The United States became a nation in the twilight of an age when the impact of war on society in western civilization seems remarkably restrained. The historical cliché that the eighteenth century was an age of 'limited war' contains much truth. Nevertheless, war had a profound influence on American development. It shaped the nature of the first settlement – Roanoke was to be a base for Elizabethan privateers to plunder Spanish wealth in the Caribbean. The Great War for Empire was the catalyst which led to the American Revolution. American independence came from war. The United States acquired a continent and an overseas empire through combat. A sanguinary civil struggle maintained American unity. And the world leadership of the United States in the twentieth century has been based upon preponderant economic and military strength convincingly demonstrated in two world wars. Through all this, it has often been argued that American struggles have been crusades and that Americans have never fought for mere 'policy.' The conflicts of Jehovah, rather than those of Bismarck, more often have been presented as an analogy for the American experience.

It is certainly true that wars have been presented to the American people as crusades for democracy and freedom. But this does not mean that statesmen and the mass of citizens have held identical views. Vicious debates have whirled around American wars which suggest that radically divergent perceptions have been held by statesmen, advisers, legislators, observers, and common people. What has seemed a just war on liberal principles to some has seemed reactionary and criminal piracy to others. What has seemed judicious policy to some has seemed misguided romanticism to their critics. But the leaders of the United States who have confronted the decision to employ force have had to judge by their insight and information. They have often believed themselves possessed of special talents and knowledge. They have also recognized that what would gain popular support may not be what they would or did recommend as policy. Whatever their views, it is safe to say that American leaders have consistently placed the independence and survival of their nation as first priorities.

This study examines Thomas Jefferson's views of war with the last thought in mind. The beliefs of Jefferson and his generation remain of fundamental importance for an understanding of American encounters with war. These men established institutions and set precedents in the relationship of force and policy which have been held as timeless models. They engaged in debates over the control and use of power. Seldom does power seem as dangerous as during war, and in light of recent analysis of the 'imperial presidency,' the Jeffersonian experience seems pertinent and instructive. Jefferson did not put his views of war down in a systematic manner. As with so many other threads of his thought, his ideas on war must be disentangled from his written work. His comments on the subject were often made at random or buried in letters and papers addressing quite different topics. To structure Jefferson's thought too rigorously would do violence to its eclectic and encyclopaedic nature. Hence a narrative approach seems best, since Jefferson's thought on war developed as he witnessed and participated in the conflicts of his time, and his attitudes varied with circumstances and his own position.

Any writer incurs many debts which can be but marginally repaid by printed acknowledgements. The book has been published with the help of a grant from the Canadian Federation for the Humanities, using funds provided by the Social Sciences and Humanities Research Council of Canada, and a grant from the Andrew W. Mellon Foundation to the University of Toronto Press. The University of Prince Edward Island provided a leave for the doctoral research upon which this work is based and funds for typing. The University of Florida proved a generous host by providing financial support, a fine library with a helpful staff, and the stimulating advice of Professor John K. Mahon and other scholars in the History Department. The encouragement of Professors Thomas Spira of the University of Prince Edward Island and A.M.J. Hyatt of the University of Western Ontario was heartening. Finally, the labour, criticism, and support of my wife, Penelope, were indispensable. All these, and others, must share in any credit this book might receive for adding to our knowledge of the past.

REGINALD C. STUART
University of Prince Edward Island

THE HALF-WAY PACIFIST

THOMAS JEFFERSON'S VIEW OF WAR

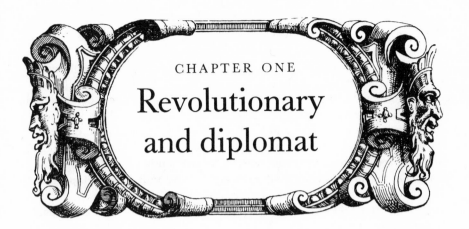

CHAPTER ONE

Revolutionary and diplomat

As our enemies have found we can reason like men, so now let us show them we can fight like men also. JEFFERSON

It should ever be held in mind that insult and war are the consequence of a want of respectability in the national character. JEFFERSON[1]

Thomas Jefferson's view of war arose from three basic sources. The first was that complex matrix of ideas, experience, and expectation which shaped the political thought of most reflective Americans of the revolutionary era. Radical whig ideology, the tenets of the Enlightenment, with its emphasis on reason, progress, and humanity, and colonial history all blended with the stimulation of the imperial crises of the 1760s. This sent Jefferson, along with the majority of colonial Americans, down the road to resistance, rebellion, independence, and republicanism.

Jefferson's personal predilections provide the second source for his view of war. He tried to avoid dogmatism, yet found that he was swept up by the emotions of the moment, as in the imperial crises and later, when political partisanship and the currents of the French Revolution gripped American imaginations. This led to an ambivalence towards war. He abhorred debt, and early recognized that conflict created enormous financial burdens for a society. He disliked direct personal confrontations, and thus developed a talent for indirectness in his foreign policies if the situation augured a military clash. He feared power, especially when held in his own hands, and came to see that war provides exceptional opportunities and dangers for the exercise of power by central authorities, for both monarchies and republics. Finally, he had an innate optimism, buoyed by the Enlightenment and the success of the American Revolution, which led him to hope that the impact of war might be lessened.

The third source of Jefferson's view of war can be found in the formative stages of his career – in practical experience. His decision to support the colonial protest against parliamentary authority took him into high political and diplomatic circles in America and Europe. There he saw ideals, greed, friendship, enmity, war, and peace alike harnessed in the pursuit of national survival and self-interests. He came to understand that his hopes for a rational and civilized future must be tempered. His early optimism faded as his perception of the nature of man and states grew. For example, the collapse of the French republic into a new imperialism under Napoleon convinced him that the United States was a bastion of republicanism in a hostile world of monarchism.

But as a republican patriot Jefferson understood that war was a necessary instrument of survival, and that it could even be waged in pursuit of American self-interest. Thus, he can with some justice be called a 'half-way pacifist,' because while he laboured to resolve disputes and achieve objectives peacefully he remained willing to resort to force if all such efforts failed. Still he feared a standing military, and any resort to arms meant troops at the ready. Eighteenth-century republicanism stressed a people's defence based upon a militia. A militia, however, proved unsuited to offensive actions in support of an aggressive foreign policy, as Jefferson later discovered. Ideology, rationalism, national ambition and self-interest, and the realities of the world at large combined in Jefferson's thought in such a way that he was never able to resolve the contradictions inherent in a resort to force even by an enlightened republican patriot.

Jefferson's first confrontation with war occurred with the advent of the movement for colonial independence which developed from resistance to the British parliamentary measures of the 1760s. As a Virginia burgess in 1774, he draughted instructions to the Virginia delegates in the new Continental Congress. These were later reprinted as a 'Summary View of the Rights of the Colonies' and gained Jefferson considerable notoriety, including proscription by George III. Jefferson argued that resistance to the king's troops was justified if they refused to submit to colonial laws, because then they could be treated as a hostile and invading force.[2] Many in both Virginia and Congress agreed, but they anticipated British military aggression with decidedly mixed emotions. Jefferson, and most colonial Americans, were reluctant revolutionaries.

The skirmish at Lexington on 19 April 1775 was an imperial catharsis. Massachusetts' governor Thomas Gage had seized colonial military stores in September of the previous year without an incident. But, on that April morning, the Massachusetts militia had gathered in a belligerent, if uncertain, mood.[3] Once the 'battle' and running fire-fight back to Boston had taken place, postriders spread the news. The tragedy, with its few casualties, was converted into an Armageddon: as the colonists heard it, innocent Americans had been brutally slaughtered by savage military mercenaries in a horrid massacre.[4] Jefferson, along with many others, was outraged, but he accepted the fact of war with an air approaching nonchalance: 'You will before this have heard that the war is now heartily entered into, without a prospect of accomodation but thro' the effectual interposition of arms.'[5] Jefferson did not seem more than momentarily concerned about the fact that a civil war had begun within the British Empire.

Congress employed Jefferson as a member of a committee to justify the *de facto* war. He had few doubts about the necessity of armed resistance. Men must lay aside thoughts of private profit to join the common cause. He expressed his personal determination: 'As our enemies have found we can reason like men, so now let us show them we can fight like men also.'[6] Turning to the work of the committee, Jefferson saw the question of the justice and necessity of the war closely linked with the nature of government. He defended the war much as he defended colonial liberties in his 'Summary View,' and in both cases contributed to the developing American republicanism.

Jefferson went straight to the point. He stated that because Britain's legislature had attempted to establish absolute rule by force of arms, a response in kind had been both necessary and just. He then traced colonial history to show that American affection for both Britain and her king had paled before the assertion of parliamentary superiority. Arbitrary taxation, the closure of the port of Boston, the transportation of defendants beyond their native colonies, and the general attempt to 'erect a despotism of unlimited extent' completed the justification for resistance. Colonial protests had been ignored and, worse, troops had invaded Massachusetts, assaulted the colonials at Lexington and Concord, and laid waste to property. The 'ministerial army' was the aggressor. Americans would be 'perfidious to posterity' to submit tamely to such injustice. They had, therefore, taken up arms for defence against 'actual violation,' and not for conquest or aggression.[7]

This was a classic case for the just war which had roots as deep as St Augustine's two cities. It also suggested that Jefferson saw war as a limited instrument, to achieve specific ends.[8] In this sense, his defence of the war for American independence was in the mainstream of the eighteenth century as

well as the much older tradition of the just war. Jefferson's developing republican ideology, which built upon the whig tradition embracing government
by consent and the compact theory of government, also lay behind his conviction that this was a just war. Clearly, the 'Declaration on Taking Up Arms'
was a work of propaganda, intended for domestic consumption and to evaporate the doubt that would inevitably have condensed in colonial minds over
armed resistance against legal authority. It was not likely to sway the English
ministry, although Jefferson and the members of Congress may have hoped
that it would.

John Dickinson concurred with the thrust of Jefferson's argument, although he thought his Virginia colleague's language was too mild. The pun-
gency of the final document, as adopted by Congress on 6 July 1775, owed
much to his own forceful prose. Once adopted, the 'Declaration' not only
reflected the views of the committee, it also represented the majority opinion
of the delegates. While it was true that these men had been elected and could
be recalled or cast down by their constituents, at this critical juncture they
had the power to commit the British Empire to civil war. Subsequently, Congress allowed letters of marque and reprisal to be issued to privateers, and established courts for the disposition of prizes.[9] On the basis of his record, one
can safely assume that Jefferson supported such measures. The right to make
war is one of the primary prerogatives of a sovereign body, and Congress, by
its actions, clearly assumed that it was a sovereign government, even before it
declared independence.

The emotional and political significance of the Declaration of Independence has served to obscure the fact that it rested on the colonial belief in the
justice of a defensive war as well as on whig ideology. War evidently had a
radicalizing logic of its own. In August 1775 Jefferson, caught up in the heat
of the moment, wrote that he would lend his hand to sink Great Britain
rather than submit. Three months later he stated: 'After the colonies have
drawn the sword there is but one step more they can take.'[10] War had forced
a choice on many colonists, whatever their partisan views, and helped to propel them towards republican autonomy as an alternative to continued colonial dependence.

The Declaration of Independence was a further justification of the war as
well as an explanation for separatism. It linked the justice of a defensive war
against tyranny with the right of revolution. Because of the self-evident
truths, because of man's natural rights, because of the rights of people in society, because of the ends of government, men could wage a defensive war
against aggression, even from their own government. This too flowed from St
Augustine, ran through the medieval legists, into the Renaissance via both

clerical and secular writers, and on into the eighteenth century sustained by Hugo Grotius, John Locke, Thomas Hobbes, and Emerich de Vattel, among others.[11] Jefferson stood at the end of a long line of tradition about war, as well as political theory, when he stated that George III had 'abdicated Government' and declared Americans 'out of his Protection' by waging war on them. 'He has plundered our seas, ravaged our Coasts, burned our towns, and destroyed the Lives of our people.' In conducting this unlawful war, the king had forced Americans to bear arms against their fellows, incited domestic insurrection in the colonies, and resorted to savage warfare on the frontiers by enlisting Indians as allies. Congress, representing the people of the United States, now had 'full Power to levy War, conclude Peace' and assume all sovereign powers. In truth, this was stating the obvious. Civil resistance had become by turns rebellion and revolution.

At first Jefferson did not experience much of the direct impact of the war between England and her rebellious colonies. The military campaigns were in the north, in New York, New Jersey, and Pennsylvania. Jefferson anticipated a short war and turned his attention to issues of domestic political reform. He might have agreed, at that time, with the inscription on the tomb of Henry III in Westminster Abbey which reads: 'Dulce bellum inexpertis – War is delightful to the unexperienced'; but he would have found a later remark by Emerson more apposite: 'War disorganizes, but it is to reorganize.'[12]

Despite his moral commitment, Jefferson expected that the war would be conducted in a civilized manner. He was enraged when he learned of Indians allied with loyalist battalions and British regulars on the frontier. Forest warfare had always been brutal, and the Revolution saw no break in this tradition. But Jefferson was oblivious of this fact and saw only the atrocities and the British efforts to create terror by using savage allies. He wanted Indian territory invaded, and more: 'I would never cease pursuing them while one of them remained on this side of the Mississippi. So unprovoked an attack and so treacherous a one should never be forgiven while one of them remains near enough to do us injury.'[13] Actually, neither loyalists nor revolutionaries had a monopoly on virtue when it came to atrocity in frontier fighting, but Jefferson fell prey to a natural tendency in wartime to attribute sin to the opposition. There was more to it than that, however, since his strong reaction flowed from genuine outrage at Indian methods, which he believed violated all the canons of civilized warfare as the men of the eighteenth century understood it.[14]

Jefferson's attitude towards the treatment of prisoners also proved very much in keeping with the humane ideals of his age. 'It is for the benefit of mankind to mitigate the horrors of war as much as possible. The practice therefore of modern nations of treating captive enemies with politeness and generosity is not only delightful in contemplation but really interesting to all the world, friends foes and neutrals.'[15] No Enlightenment philosopher could have phrased it better. When General Burgoyne's surrendered Saratoga Convention Army established its camp near Jefferson's home at Charlottesville, Virginia, he spent many happy and tranquil hours with the British and German officers, who were loosely confined, enjoying good food, wine, conversation, and music. The strife of war seemed distant in such halcyon days. But the holiday atmosphere began to pass after 1 June 1779, when Jefferson became governor of Virginia.

Jefferson's initial shock over the horrors of war arose from the Henry Hamilton affair. Hamilton commanded British forces in the Detroit region and had freely employed Indians. The British always tried to curb their allies, but they were seldom successful. Certainly, Hamilton's Indians were guilty of indiscretions, to say the least. When he was forced to surrender to George Rogers Clark and Virginia troops, Hamilton found that Jefferson had a streak of Hammurabi in his soul. Restraint was thrust aside as Hamilton was cast in irons for exciting the Indians to their 'usual circumstances of barbarity.' Jefferson made it clear that he saw a dramatic distinction between 'civilized' and 'savage' warfare: 'On a dispasionate examination we trust it must furnish a contemplation rather pleasing to the generous Soldier to see his honourable bravery respected even by those against whom it happen to be inlisted, and discriminated from the cruel and cowardly warfare of the savage whose object in war is to extinguish human nature.'[16]

Jefferson's attitude stirred up a minor hornet's nest, but the governor stuck to his guns. He explained that Hamilton had capitulated and thrown himself on the generosity of his captors. Hamilton's reputation did not warrant largesse. The customarily objective and scholarly Jefferson accepted frontier rumours and assertions as proof of Hamilton's guilt. To Major General William Phillips, the commander of the Convention Army, Jefferson wrote that Hamilton was being justly kept in irons on general principles of national retaliation. It was a lesson to the British who had maltreated American prisoners, and a contrast to the benevolence extended to English soldiers by the revolutionaries. Indulging in sophistry, Jefferson argued that retaliation was an act of kindness under such circumstances. Further, Hamilton had assumed responsibility for the Indians' behaviour when he enlisted them as allies. Since they were guilty of butchery, so was he.[17]

The Hamilton affair illustrated Jefferson's view of war as a limited instrument. The object was not to destroy the enemy, but to lead him to see justice. The horrors of war should be ameliorated as much as possible, and in

Jefferson's view that was precisely what Hamilton, a man who should have known better, had not done. Jefferson reflected the civilized attitudes towards war so widely applauded by military and political leaders in the eighteenth century.

By late September 1779 the Council of Virginia advised that Hamilton be released on parole, echoing Jefferson's own view on prisoners. The conflict would not be affected by wreaking vengeance on captives but only by 'Honourable valour in the field.'[18] Jefferson was never happy about the outcome of the Hamilton affair and he continued to defend his actions, although he submitted to the council's recommendation with moderate good grace.[19] At the same time, he advocated that George Clark should attempt the 'extermination' of several tribes, or their 'removal [since] the same world will scarcely do for them and us.'[20] With both Hamilton and the Indians, Jefferson revealed that he believed strongly in the principle of retaliation.

Jefferson was momentarily alarmed when in October 1780 a British fleet appeared off Hampton Roads. He knew that supplies were low, that most of the local troops were serving in the Carolinas, that there were loyalist elements in Virginia which might assist a British landing, and that the Convention Army might be liberated *en masse*.[21] The British prisoners were hastily removed, but the emergency passed when the English fleet withdrew after a short reconnaissance.

The respite was brief. From 31 December 1780 to 26 July 1781, Virginia felt the direct ravages of war. Much of Jefferson's chagrin may have come from the charges of cowardice and incompetence levelled at him by his political enemies.[22] He even suffered personal humiliation when he was rousted out of his home by a cavalry detachment of Banastre Tarleton's legion, invading from the south. Jefferson was forced to flee, but not bolt headlong in his nightshirt as was later alleged. The invasion was no lighter a burden either because it was commanded by Benedict Arnold, whom Jefferson termed a 'parricide.' Jefferson was so enraged at Arnold that he hatched a scheme to kidnap the general so that Americans could have the satisfaction of trying and hanging the traitor, but the plot came to nothing.[23]

The British invasion created a sense of frustration in Jefferson and demoralization in Virginia. The militia responded slowly. In some instances it did not respond at all. That which did turn out behaved badly. Jefferson did not attempt to wield his authority in such cases because he had good reason to believe that if he had pressed the militia in recalcitrant counties he would have had disobedience, even mutiny, on his hands. Rather than risk an open revolt against his office, Jefferson let the matter pass.[24] This sad combination of circumstances forced him to ride out the storm of war and hope for the best.

But British behaviour provoked him again in March of 1781. The British had threatened to execute any paroled Americans found under arms. Normally, this would have been reasonable enough, since men on parole were supposed to be in a kind of limbo as far as the war was concerned. Here, however, the British had been rounding up colonials and issuing them paroles wholesale to undermine American manpower reserves. It was a clever stratagem but Jefferson threatened instant retaliation if any of these Americans were executed. Ironically, in light of his own policy towards Henry Hamilton, he stated that 'the event of this Contest will hardly be affected by the fate of a few miserable Captives in war.'[25]

Jefferson had discovered that maintaining rational and civilized behaviour in wartime is difficult at best. In keeping with the just-war tradition, he maintained that any free nation had the right to punish for injuries received, but could not exceed that.[26] He was not yet fully aware that he was becoming the citizen of a new nation-state, and that nation-states defined their own interests, accepting no authority save superior force. This rule applied to monarchies and republics alike. Self-interest and fear of punishment, not humane principles, provided the spurs to action.

In December 1783 Jefferson was on a congressional committee which suggested instructions for American ministers in Europe. The instructions betrayed the Enlightenment attitudes towards war which the Americans hoped to put into effect. Negotiators were in the future to try and secure clauses which allowed a nine-month grace for merchants to collect their debts, settle their affairs, and depart peacefully in case war arose between the contracting parties. Further, anyone on either side who laboured peacefully for the common good was not to be molested.[27] These ideas were also consistent with Jefferson's own belief that war was a limited instrument of governments, and consonant with the attitudes of conservative eighteenth-century rulers who sought to shield their productive subjects from the ravages of warfare.

In his 'Notes on the State of Virginia,' published in 1785 while Jefferson was in Paris, he suggested that war was a learned characteristic. Perhaps habit was to blame for making men 'honor force more than finesse.' But there was also a national right of self-defence: 'while an enemy is in our bowels, the first object is to expel him.'[28] Thus man and his institutions seemed the sources of war to Jefferson at this point. While reason dictated that it was never in the true interests of any nation to go to war, Jefferson knew that reason would not always prevail. Passions, habits, and commercial competition would make wars well-nigh inevitable. This was Jefferson at his analytical best, free from the emotional tentacles activated by a patriotic struggle. Jefferson believed that republics would by their very nature be pacific. The

American people would never, he was confident, embark on any other than a purely defensive war. But the United States could not hope to control the policies of other states: 'Wars then must sometimes be our lot; and all the wise can do, will be to avoid that half of them which would be produced by our own follies and our own acts of injustice; and to make for the other half the best preparations we can.'[29]

By the end of the American struggle for independence Jefferson had developed a threefold view of war. First, he saw its origins in human nature and human systems – nations and commercial intercourse. Monarchs especially were prone to make war for selfish reasons, and here he believed that institutional reforms such as the Americans were effecting would promote peace. Voltaire had also reviled monarchs, just as a new breed of free-trade economists was arguing that reducing mercantilistic barriers would reduce international friction and promote peace. Second, Jefferson believed that some war was inevitable. But it was no excuse for barbarism, however unavoidable it was from time to time. Therefore, the goal should be restraint in war, rather than outright elimination. His optimism and pessimism seemed evenly balanced here. And his ideas were within the mainstream of thinking about war and peace in the eighteenth century. Finally, Jefferson saw a clear relationship between war and national policy. Nations justifiably used war to punish for wrongs received and to redress grievances. This made it an affair of governments, not of peoples, and its object was justice, not conquest. This idea too was consistent with the just-war tradition. While many Americans may have seen the war for independence as a crusade, Jefferson had not. He had been committed and occasionally angry, but he had seldom forgotten for long that the objects of war were specific and limited – to redress injuries inflicted by the British ministry and then seek recognition of independence from the crown. Even the burgeoning republican ideology among leading Americans meant only that such wars were consciously related more closely to the interests of the people. Republicanism did nothing to change the nature of war.

Jefferson's tour of duty as a minister plenipotentiary stationed in Paris reinforced these ideas. He was keenly aware of the implications for America of the many European wars which threatened. Shortly after arriving in France, Jefferson thought a war was brewing between Holland, supported by Prussia, and Austria. He wrote theatrically that 'the lamp of war is kindled here, not to be extinguished but by torrents of blood,' fully expecting a virtual Armageddon to break loose at any moment. In 1787 problems over the Bavarian succession threatened to involve France in a war with Great Britain. If the terms of the Alliance of 1778 came into force, where the United States had guaranteed the French West Indies, America could be exposed to British attack. When war erupted between Russia and Turkey, the major powers avoided the vortex, restrained by internal dissension and depleted treasuries, although Jefferson had fully expected the conflict to sweep in all of Europe.[30]

These perennial spasms gave Jefferson perennial trembles. In common with many of his fellow Americans, he viewed Europe and its monarchs as a fount of war and feared that the fragile United States would be badly, even fatally, damaged were it to be drawn into a major conflict. He refrained from asking for French aid to lever the British out of the northwest posts in case the French insisted on further American assurances about their West Indies in exchange.[31]

Jefferson continued to fear that America's foreign commerce could cause international difficulties, and that these in turn might threaten war. While the United States would be neutral in any European conflict, the great maritime nations – Britain, France, and Spain – would not permit free trade with their enemies. Incidents would inevitably arise, because America was then committed to liberal principles regarding neutral rights, especially the doctrine of 'free ships, free goods.' Although American statesmen would later abandon this principle as impractical and ineffectual given international circumstances and attitudes, at this time Jefferson saw an inevitable clash if Americans maintained their commerce and their principles simultaneously. Thus he was privately prepared to see the United States shut off from the world, like China, because that would be the most effective way to avoid wars.[32] But he readily admitted that his countrymen had a taste for trade, and his mission, after all, was to negotiate commercial treaties with the Europeans. So he bent every effort to enlarge trade with France to counterbalance what he viewed as an unhealthy dependence upon Britain. He kept his private convictions and public actions in separate compartments over this matter.

Since Americans would not give up their commerce, their government would have to be prepared to defend their rights:

... property will be violated on the sea and in foreign ports, their persons will be insulted, emprisoned &c, for pretended debts, contracts, crimes &c &c. These insults must be resented, even if we had no feelings, yet to prevent their eternal repetition. Or in other words, our commerce on the oceans and in other countries must be paid for by frequent war. The justest dispositions possible in ourselves will not secure us against it.[33]

Jefferson was unduly pessimistic. Trade disputes are usually settled amicably. But he knew that neutral carriers often reap windfall profits during wartime, and Jefferson believed that such temptations would divert Americans from their true concerns and subvert their republican virtue, as surely as they would threaten American autonomy.[34] Although Jefferson worked to further America's foreign trade, even declaring later that it was a handmaiden to agriculture, he was never truly comfortable about its potential for creating international disorder.

Jefferson became thoroughly convinced that Americans must pay off their debts as a high priority. This stemmed from his private financial difficulties. 'The torment of mind I endure till the moment shall arrive when I shall not owe a shilling on earth is such as really to render life of little value.'[35] Such a statement was Jeffersonian hyperbole and may have been written at a time when he was more concerned than usual about his perpetually shaky finances. But this personal concern easily became the foundation for public policy in his mind. Americans must pursue neutrality, he argued, because the debts from the last war must be discharged before accepting any new burdens.[36] As president, Jefferson was consumed with a desire to avoid further debt and his administration became noted for the stringent economic measures designed by Albert Gallatin to balance the budget, especially by reducing military expenditures.

The concern with debt was linked with yet another facet of Jefferson's philosophy – the concept that the earth belonged to the living. He developed the idea, buttressed by some abstruse calculations and unconvincing assertions, that the generations of mankind were somehow discrete, and that both the form and conduct of public policy could be shaped with this in mind. One generation had no right to bind the next by contracting debts beyond its immediate ability to pay.[37] Monarchs, because of their arbitrary power to make war and to tax, saddled their subjects with mountains of accumulating debt down through successive generations. The possible war between Holland and Austria moved Jefferson to write: 'Blessed effect of kingly government, where a pretended insult to the sister of a king is to produce the wanton sacrifice of a hundred or two thousand of the people who have entrusted themselves to his government, and as many of his enemies! And we think our's a bad government.'[38]

The American Constitution had circumvented this problem from the start by placing the war power in the legislature. But Americans could go one step further by adopting the notion of discrete generations. This would '... exclude at the threshold of our new government the contagious and ruinous errors of this quarter of the globe, which have armed despots with means, not sanctioned by nature, for binding in chains their fellow men. We have already given in example one effectual check to the Dog of War by transferring the power of letting him loose from the Executive to the Legislative body, from those who are to spend to those who are to pay.'[39] A republican form of government, where the war teeth of the executive were blunted, if not wholly drawn because of the president's powers as commander-in-chief, would lessen the likelihood of war. This view was based on a faith in progress, in republicanism, and in the sound judgement of the mass of people. It also reflected a recurrent American belief in institutional solutions to social problems.[40]

But there were occasions when Jefferson judged that war would be the best policy. A case in point was the Barbary pirates. In 1784 he learned that Algerian corsairs had seized an American merchant ship and crew for ransom. He believed that a purchased peace would be too costly. The United States should offer a treaty, and if Algiers spurned this, then 'why not go to war with them?' Other European governments found the Algerians a nagging problem, so the Americans might find willing allies. Such a struggle would not be difficult, he believed. Victory could come from simple commerce raids.[41] 'The motives pleading for war rather than tribute are numerous and honourable, those opposing them are mean and shortsighted ...' A naval force could be built which would later serve as a 'bridle' in the mouths of the West Indian powers, and improve the American image in Europe. A weak response to Algiers would evoke foreign contempt. This would 'inevitably bring on insults which must involve us in war. A coward is much more exposed to quarrels than a man of spirit.'[42]

Jefferson's argument for a limited war of policy against Algiers flowed from his rising nationalism. The credit in the vault of national pride would more than compensate for expenses by the treasury. And if the Americans wished to maintain a free commerce, then they must take pains to show that their country had unity and energy.[43] If European governments had more respect for the United States, this would expedite the negotiation of commercial treaties, and therefore encourage peace. 'It should ever be held in mind that insult and war are the consequences of a want of respectability in the national character.'[44]

Jefferson was also thinking of building a deterrent, for he commented that the United States would never be safe until 'our magazines are filled with arms.'[45] He was of course not arguing for a large standing force, but merely for stockpiles to service the militia.[46] Given sufficient time, he believed that the Americans could make themselves largely invulnerable. The real deterrence in Jefferson's mind comprised republican enthusiasm, a vigorous militia, a small navy, geographic isolation, American resources, and adequate taxing and war-making powers delegated to a stronger central government.

Jefferson's assertion that war was the best way to deal with the Algerians thus flowed from many beliefs. His London colleague, John Adams, disagreed, arguing that tribute and ransom were better, since the United States was in no position to wage a war. Jefferson maintained that war would be cheaper in the long run because it would not only deal with Algiers but also impress the other Barbary pirates.[47] He even suggested a possible league for peace. The American commissioners had approached the French government to inquire if, when France's current treaty with Algiers expired, his most Christian majesty contemplated war. If so, Congress would probably favour an alliance rather than treat with powers which so 'barbarously and inhumanely commence hostilities against others who have done them no injury.'[48]

The French demurred and Jefferson pondered multilateral rather than bilateral arrangements. Portugal, Naples, perhaps even Russia, might co-operate. America could furnish a 'couple of frigates,' establish a convention, and mount cruises on the Algerian coast.[49] Jefferson had the smaller states in mind here. They had more to gain because their smaller merchant fleets felt losses more keenly and they lacked both the military and financial muscles to obtain favourable terms from the pirates on their own. Jefferson's scheme bore a close resemblance to the Enlightenment peace plans which began to emerge in the late seventeenth century. The several powers at war with Algiers would confederate and force a peace without tribute. Their ambassadors at the Court of Versailles would form a directing council. No war between the partners would disrupt the enterprise, and once Algiers had been coerced the parties would train their guns on the other Barbary pirates if they did not agree to treat.[50] Jefferson enlisted the aid of the Marquis de Lafayette, who formally requested the American Congress to consider this proposal.[51]

A motion in Congress of July 1787 actually directed Jefferson to form such a confederacy.[52] John Jay, secretary for foreign affairs, thought that it would 'always be more for the Honor and Interest of the United States to prefer War to Tribute,' and he believed that the Americans had the resources for the enterprise. But Jay agreed with John Adams that the country was unprepared for a war of any kind and therefore, with 'great Regret,' he advised against making any commitment.[53] So the motion remained a paper decision.

The idea fared little better in Europe. The Comte de Vergennes, the French foreign minister, told Lafayette to drop the scheme, Spain declined to receive it, and while some smaller powers, such as Portugal, Naples, Venice, and Sweden, were sympathetic, they would do nothing without a guarantee of non-interference from France. This the French would not grant. The idea of a league to enforce peace, even in such a minor way as this, was an idea whose time had not yet come. But Jefferson's ideas and actions put him in the mainstream of the thinking of the age of limited war. The peace plans of the

Abbé Saint Pierre, Jean-Jacques Rousseau, Jeremy Bentham, and Immanuel Kant were more ambitious, but little different in conception or operation from that mapped out here by Jefferson.[54] All argued for a confederation as a directing body and all accepted the efficacy of war to produce peace.

As a diplomat, Jefferson attempted to implement other aspects of Enlightenment thinking on war and peace. The 'model treaty' of 1776, which was a general guide for American negotiators, stated in part that '... all fishermen, all cultivators of the earth, and all artisans or manufacturers, unarmed, and inhabiting unfortified towns, villages or places, who labour for the common benefit and subsistence of mankind, and peaceably following their respective employments, shall be allowed to continue the same, and shall not be molested ...'[55] in the event that war broke out between contracting parties. The Americans were attempting to institutionalize one of the fundamental tenets of limited war – that war was between governments and not peoples. Further, its effects on mankind were to be cushioned as much as possible. How extensively the Americans drew directly from Vattel, Christian Wolff, Samuel Pufendorf, or the other codifiers of international law is problematical at best. But there is convincing evidence that Jefferson and his colleagues were broadly familiar with the thinking of their age on the origins and conduct of war.[56]

Jefferson drew up a model treaty of his own while in France, adding to the particulars developed by Congress. First, he wanted all goods free to avoid interference with neutral commerce. Second, if contracting parties went to war, their trade and husbandry should not be interrupted, prisoners were to be well treated, and merchants were to be allowed time to settle their affairs and depart from enemy territory peacefully. And Jefferson added women, children, and scholars to the list of non-combatants.[57] The link with the Enlightenment and the age of limited war could not be more clear.

These ideas might have remained little more than the fruits of an academic exercise had they not found their way into treaties actually negotiated and ratified. The treaty with Prussia was most significant in this regard. The American commissioners noted that the proposed articles should commend themselves to the king of Prussia because by softening the calamities of war they were in favour of humanity.[58] By the original law of nations, injuries evoked war and extirpation. By degrees, however, war had been humanized. Slavery replaced death as fair treatment for prisoners. Why should such progress not continue? Why not in future exempt certain classes of men from the ravages of war? After all, it was 'for the interest of humanity in general, that the occasions of war, and the inducements to it should be diminished.' If rapine were prohibited, 'one of the encouragements to war is taken away, and peace therefore more likely to continue and be lasting.'[59] Articles XXIII and

XXIV in the final treaty dealt explicitly with these points. Such provisions seem almost poignant to a twentieth-century mind, reflecting a naïveté, albeit noble, which runs directly contrary to our experience with war since Jefferson's time. But the Americans were sincere and reflected the best ideals of their age when they attempted institutionally to restrict the impact of war on society.

Offsetting Jefferson's faith that the ravages of war could be softened was the nagging knowledge that war could also be a useful instrument of national policy. His Enlightenment ideals were always present, but they receded when questions of national independence and security arose. A demonstrated readiness for war constituted a deterrent. However hopeful, men in the Enlightenment were usually fundamentallly pessimistic about man and war. John Jay once wrote: 'While there are knaves and fools in the world, there will be wars in it; and that nations should make war against nations is less surprising than their living in uninterrupted peace and harmony.'[60] Even a league to enforce peace depended upon war, after all, to secure its ends. Jefferson's pessimism was seldom as baldly stated as this, but it was always there. And Jefferson continued to see foreign trade as a danger, equal to the vagaries of European politics and man's flawed nature. He still argued that military coercion was the best policy against weak opponents, although he seemed more cautious when dealing with the big powers of his time. National pride had become important to him, no less so than independence, since the two were interrelated and linked with the future of republicanism. By the end of the 1780s, then, it was clear that Jefferson had adopted the prevailing attitudes of enlightened eighteenth-century opinion towards war.

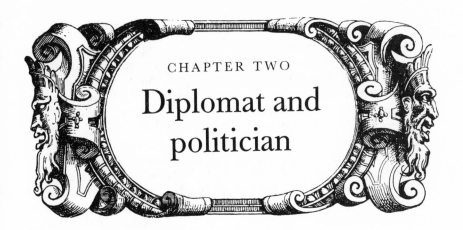

CHAPTER TWO

Diplomat and politician

War is now seldom entered into but upon necessities of State which render it unavoidable; and it is prosecuted with a degree of temperance and humanity which does our age honour. THOMAS BARNARD

The insults & injuries committed on us by both the belligerent parties, from the beginning of 1793 to this day, & still continuing, cannot now be wiped off by engaging in war with one of them. JEFFERSON[1]

When Jefferson returned to the United States from his diplomatic tour overseas, he became his nation's first secretary of state. He was reluctant to accept the post but acceded out of personal loyalty to Washington and his own interest in the future of the United States. He subsequently became embroiled in political controversy because of his strong French proclivities, first within the cabinet which evolved during Washington's terms as president, and second in the country at large as the first political parties coalesced. In the 1790s it was common for political antagonists to rush to the intellectual barricades by pamphleteering. The French Revolution aroused political passions in American breasts second only to those of their own revolution against British rule and these found frequent outlets in print. Champions of liberal republicanism ranged themselves against conservative defenders of order and property, particularly after the execution of Louis XVI and the onset of the Terror. Jefferson suffered excoriation by writers who were convinced that his sympathies for France jeopardized the future of the United States. But he was far too much of a nationalist to wed the future of his country to the fortunes of any single European power, even a republican France. While he had a deep empathy with France's struggle for liberty, he was guided more by his belief that a counterpoise to the weight of Great Britain was needed in American foreign relations. When the revolutionary wars began in Europe, Jefferson welcomed them, accepting a republican war against monarchy as just almost by definition, but he never argued for American participation in the maelstrom.[2]

Jefferson's tour abroad left him highly sensitive to the vicissitudes and permutations of European politics. As early as April 1790 he noted the likelihood of another war in northern Europe and suggested that as a result American wheat would have an excellent market. By early May his European correspondents had begun to write about a crisis between England and Spain. Zealous Spanish officers had seized English traders in Nootka Sound, on the coast of Vancouver Island on the far western side of North America. The English demanded restitution, reparation, and simultaneously threatened war.[3]

The American secretary of state hoped that 'peace and profit' would be the American share in the conflict but at the same time he was concerned lest France be drawn in. The treaties of 1778 might prove embarrassing to the Americans and threaten war with England. But he still was dazzled by images of high prices and good markets, thinking that these might be sufficient to allow the United States to discharge all public and private debts. He sounded parasitic when he hoped that the 'new world will fatten on the follies of the old,' but was more to the point when he added that if they could maintain neutrality then Americans 'must become the carriers for all parties.' Jefferson's vision was no fantasy since American merchants reaped massive profits throughout the European wars from 1793 to 1815. The Quasi-War against France, Jefferson's embargo of 1807-8, and the War of 1812 produced the only dips in an otherwise steady upward trend.[4] Jefferson's overall strategy was to have America use her neutrality like a belle uses her charms and have the rivals bid for her favours.[5] This involved a subtle and fragile line of policy, however, based on the none-too-safe assumption that the rivals would consider American charms sufficiently alluring. In reality, the policy proved to be a tightrope walk, with no net.

Jefferson attempted to put his ideas on deterrence into practice. He still argued that whatever enabled Americans to go to war would secure their peace.[6] He was convinced that the United States was strong enough to give European powers pause, which he hoped would lead to concessions favouring American interests. In the Nootka Sound affair he relied on the whims and caprices of European politics, plus artful diplomacy, to produce such concessions. He had a particular interest in the west, which was threatened by the prospect of an Anglo-Spanish clash. Americans had been moving into the interior in a steady stream since the end of the Revolution and were reaching sufficient numbers to be both politically effective and diplomatically dangerous.

Jefferson was certain that the western territories held by Spain would eventually fall into the American lap by default. But free navigation on the Mississippi was imperative in the interim. One day, he mused, westerners would not tolerate being shut up by the Spanish any longer. Then they would rebel, and the best policy for the United States would be to take whatever Spanish territory proved necessary by force of arms.[7] Such an argument was hypothetical, but reasonable in terms of the American future, and it shows that Jefferson was prepared to argue for a war to sustain what he believed were national interests. The Nootka Sound affair seemed to present an opportunity to Jefferson to nudge destiny a trifle. He instructed William Short, the American minister in Paris, to seek out Lafayette. He wanted to have France pressure Spain when the Anglo-Spanish war broke out. Spain should be told that she would find America ranged against her if she would not agree to a definitive boundary settlement. To Spain herself, Jefferson was downright belligerent. But the Nootka Sound affair did not erupt in war. Jefferson's scheme fell to dust as the Spanish bowed to English demands.[8]

America had to wait for Spanish territory, but the Nootka Sound affair did elicit Jefferson's fears for America's future. Had a war developed, the British would likely have marched troops overland from Canada to take Spanish Louisiana and Florida. Jefferson was convinced to the point of an obsession that Britain was ruled by principles of conquest, colonization, commerce, monopoly, and revenge. If she established such a cordon around the United States, America's future lot would be 'bloody and eternal war; or indissoluble confederacy' with Britain. Jefferson wrote to the American minister in London that the United States viewed any prospective transfer of territory on her borders as gravely serious.[9] The cabinet agreed since Jefferson expressed majority opinion, and while the American protest was real it was also partly bluster. Alexander Hamilton exposed this through his close connection with George Beckwith, a British secret agent. Lord Grenville, the British foreign secretary, was thus always fully informed about American policy. When the American minister, Gouverneur Morris, hinted that the Americans did not want to go to war over the evacuation of the northwest posts but knew their rights and would *avail themselves of them when time and circumstances may suit*,' Grenville knew that this was sheer bravado.[10] The British were unwilling to push the United States into belligerency and Beckwith's Hamiltonian pipeline told them precisely how far they could go.

Jefferson's perception of the link between war and policy found some application during the cabinet discussions over the implications of the Nootka Sound crisis for the United States. Washington asked how the government should respond if the British did ask to move troops through American territory. If it seemed that Louisiana were about to fall under British control, Jefferson wanted the United States to become a party 'in the *general war* expected to take place, should this be the only means of preventing the calamity.' He would not deny the British outright; rather he would stall for time, hoping that circumstances developed favourably. The Americans would not be able to prevent the British from moving through by force. To refuse and have passage occur anyway would mean that the United States would have to enter the war immediately or 'pocket an acknowledged insult in the face of the world; and one insult pocketed soon produces another.'[11] If the British passed without asking leave, then Jefferson counselled a protest to keep the issue alive until events determined whether peace or war would better suit the American interest. Despite this evasive policy, he was intensely suspicious of the British and would have been prepared to fight rather than see the United States surrounded by her arch enemy.

The Anglo-Spanish war never materialized so all this speculation on Jefferson's part remained purely hypothetical. But the crisis revealed genuine fears and the basic principles guiding Jefferson's view of foreign policy, and hence of war. Clearly the national interest was paramount. It seems reasonable to conclude that Jefferson saw war and peace as the obverse and reverse sides of a coin to be used to purchase advantage for the United States. He was neither a scheming Machiavellian nor a pacifist, but a staunch nationalist working in what he thought was the best interest of his country. When he learned that the war scare had blown away, Jefferson concluded that while there would have been good prices a war 'would have exposed us to risks also, which are better deferred, for some years at least.'[12] Jefferson was convinced that time would work in favour of the United States. A policy of avoiding entanglement and war was thus the most sensible. Like a Marxist, Jefferson thought in long-range terms with the conviction that history was on his side.

Jefferson attempted to influence American policy towards the Barbary states consistent with his initial reactions to the prospect of paying tribute. He resurrected his perpetual cruise idea mounted by a confederacy of powers. He argued that it would not be costly and Congress now had the ability to raise adequate funding for the scheme. He presented his ideas in a series of papers on American commercial and diplomatic relations. The case for paying tribute was included, but Jefferson made it clear that he still thought war a better policy. It would cost little more than was being lost on high insurance rates and captured cargoes. He even suggested that Muslims could be taken captive in a counter-war to exchange for Americans. But there was no support for such a policy in Congress and Jefferson shelved his plans once again.[13] America did not wage a war of policy against the pirates until Jefferson became president.

Jefferson's belligerent attitude towards Spain did not evaporate with the Anglo-Spanish crisis. He instructed the American minister in Madrid to warn Spain that continued frontier incidents in America might propel the two countries into a war. This was a pressure tactic since Jefferson wrote to a Kentucky official that the central government would brook no trespassing on its prerogatives in war and peace. Jefferson turned in the opposite direction a year later when he suggested that the United States might sound Spain on the possibility of an alliance against the Barbary states. Evidently Jefferson did not cavil at suggesting two lines of policy which seemed strongly contradictory, but he caromed in the other direction again. He asked to be apprized by the American negotiators if Spain seemed unlikely to agree to a friendly settlement so that the United States would 'no longer be tied up by principles which ... would be inconsistent with duty & self-preservation.'[14]

Jefferson's equivocating can be explained in part because he saw war and peace as tools of policy. Whichever he thought would better serve American interests of the moment tended to find his support. While he believed that Americans abhorred conquest on principle because of their republicanism, he was also an expansionist. Jefferson did not confuse force with right, a fault he attributed to European statesmen, but he had a habit of calling all American interests in Mississippi navigation 'rights.' Jefferson was more pacific towards the Indians, but still hoped they would get a good drubbing for frontier depredations. He saw military defeat as a prelude to peace, as he did with the Barbary states, but then thought that the Indians could be pacified by 'liberal & constant presents.' He had an eye on the English and Spanish method here. Unlike the greedy Barbary pirates, purchased peace with the Indians would be cheap. The expense of St Clair's expedition in 1791 'would have served for presents for half a century.'[15]

American interests and expense thus explain the apparent inconsistency in Jefferson's policies with the Indians and the pirates. Removed now from the passions of the War for Independence, Jefferson saw the Indians as uncorrupted in their wilderness home. And peace would further '... leave no pretext for raising or continuing an army. Every rag of an Indian depredation will otherwise serve as a ground to raise troops with those who think a standing army and a public debt necessary for the happiness of the U.S. and we shall never be permitted to get rid of either.'[16] Thus, republican fears of standing armies, along with his political partisanship, shaped his view of correct foreign policy as the 1790s wore on. Finally, he did not accept any war against Indians as just. He once suggested that it would be preferable to 'send an armed force and make war against the intruders as being more just & less expensive.'[17]

A new element in Jefferson's approach to both foreign policy and his view of war was the possibility of commercial interdiction as a substitute for the use of armed force in a crisis. Although a vociferous agrarian, he had gained a keen, and perhaps exaggerated, sense of the importance and potential power of American commerce during his years abroad. When he saw the extent of American trade with Britain, he thought he saw a nascent weapon. Jefferson had always viewed treaties from a commercial rather than a political perspective, and he swam in the mainstream of the free-trade thought that swelled during the era of the American Revolution. Faced with English discrimination after 1783, he came to the conclusion that equal retaliation might pry open closed and desirable markets.[18]

This thinking was interrelated with the whole question of Anglo-American relations, which grew stormy and complex once war commenced in Europe. As Alexander Hamilton was quick to point out, any economic action on America's part would have meant a tacit alliance with Britain's enemies and a compromise of American neutrality. Jefferson was thinking of using economic force as a means to maintain a balance of power, which he was convinced would work in America's favour. But he wanted to substitute commerce for warships, armies, and bribes to maintain such a balance. The English grew increasingly sensitive to the prospect of American pressure, however, as they revealed when they sent George Hammond as an accredited minister to replace the unofficial Beckwith. Disagreement between Hamilton and Jefferson over the current policy to follow with Britain was an important factor in the formation of political parties and in the crystallization of Jefferson's own partisanship.

A new danger clearly arose in 1793 when revolutionary France declared war on the monarchies of Europe in the name of liberty. This era of war, which would last until 1815, tore the fabric of belief in limited war to shreds. Jefferson, along with many others of his time, was confident that war could be controlled, but the power of mass ideology transformed wars between states into crusades. The new conflicts were between peoples, not just governments.

Jefferson was engulfed in the enthusiasm generated by the war for liberty in Europe. 'May heaven favor your cause,' he wrote to Lafayette in June of 1792.[19] When he heard that the Prussian army had been defeated by the cannons at Valmy, Jefferson was jubilant and hoped the event would be 'followed by some proper catastrophe on them.' But he did not want America to join any crusades. Although it would be a 'disagreeable pill to our friends' neutrality was necessary.[20] Jefferson's sense of republican solidarity was intellectual and emotional, but not political. He also believed that Americans did not want war, and, while they would probably not stifle their affections or desires, he hoped that 'they will suppress the effects of them so as to preserve a fair neutrality.'[21]

Jefferson was overly sanguine in this regard. The partisanship of Americans was dangerous to the point of challenge to authority. Hamilton saw a possible clash with England and urged that the French treaties of 1778 be cast aside, but Jefferson would not hear of it. Treaties must be scrupulously honoured unless there was a 'great, inevitable & imminent' danger. The United States was not obliged to enter the fray under any terms of those treaties, but if America ignored them this could give France a just cause for war. Jefferson cited Grotius, Pufendorf, Wolff, and Vattel to buttress his opinion. Still, there was a limit. Nations only preserved their good faith until their own survival was in the balance.[22] Washington issued a proclamation of neutrality, despite Hamilton's opposition, and Jefferson did his best to have it fairly administered.

The furore created by the activities of Edmond Genet, the Girondist minister who tried to drag the United States into the conflict in Europe, revealed facets of Jefferson's view of war, as well as his devotion to American neutrality. Jefferson still saw war as an instrument used by governments, not peoples, despite his enthusiasm. He was an American nationalist first and a republican ideologue second, even though he asserted in the summer of 1793 that events in Europe were of immense importance for the future of 'mankind all over the earth, and not a little so to ours.'[23] Jefferson knew that partisanship could tear the country apart and that financial ruin could ensue if war came. His political conception of war emerged in his response to the enlistment of Americans on French privateers. Individuals had no right to go to war on their own since the war power lay with Congress under the terms of the Constitution. Neither the law nor the 'general principles of society' allowed individuals to make up their own minds in this regard.[24]

The wars of the French Revolution were total wars but Jefferson remained rooted in the thought of the eighteenth century. When he first learned that the naval powers opposed to France might extend the definition of contraband to include provisions, he called this a 'justifiable cause of war.' But Jefferson hoped for commercial retaliation rather than armed reprisals as a response, since this would show 'that nations may be brought to do justice by appeals to their interests as well as by appeals to arms.'[25] He believed economic retaliation would work well, be safe, and relieve Americans of the horror of shedding blood. It would also represent progress by introducing a substitute for trial by combat into international affairs. This was the age of limited war speaking, not the age of democratic fervour which justified excess in the name of liberty. Jefferson believed that in recent times the law of nations had been liberalized by the 'refinements of manners and morals, and evidenced by the Declarations, Stipulations, and practice of every civilized nation.' Further, 'reason and usage' had established that nations which went to war left others to pursue their 'agriculture, manufactures, and other ordinary vocations ... to come and go freely, without injury or molestation.'[26] In short, war was an affair between the governments fighting. In Europe the crusading zeal aroused by the revolutionary wars shattered the edifice of limited war; in America the structure remained intact in the mind of the secretary of state.

Jefferson still sought advantages for the United States by alluding to war in his diplomacy. He wrote to the American commissioners in Spain that his countrymen were holding themselves in check over Creek depredations on the Spanish-American frontier. But Spain should be told that citizens had a right to expect protection from their government, and if peace could not be obtained by temperate measures then the United States would be compelled to go to extremes. If Spain chose to view American defence against Creek 'butchery as a cause of war to her, we must meet her also in war ...'[27] This was Jeffersonian bravado again, since he did not want war, and, as long as Spain remained close to England, American bluster meant little. Once Spain began to drift back into the French orbit and the English and Americans appeared to reach an accord with the signing of Jay's Treaty, circumstances altered, but by then Jefferson was no longer in office.

On the eve of his retirement, Jefferson presented a report on American commerce. He assumed that the British had become dependent upon American trade and that the United States could gain concessions through the use of passive force. Jefferson's idea about a substitute for war was beginning to find firmer expression. Madison had been sponsoring such measures against the English, but Hamilton and the Federalist majority had been in steadfast opposition. Temporary embargoes were enacted nevertheless and Jefferson's enthusiasm for commercial retaliation as a substitute for armed force began to mount.[28] More important, such a policy found favour with large numbers of Americans in both parties, in and out of Congress.

Jefferson retreated to Monticello when he resigned his post as secretary of state but he remained in close touch with affairs and then became tacit head of the emerging Republican party. He followed John Jay's mission to London, and while some of his neighbours seemed to think that the United States should make a 'spirited' response to English insults, he wished 'for peace, if it can be preserved, *salve fide et honore*.'[29] Jefferson's view of war and his intensifying faith in the efficacy of economic coercion were thrown into sharp relief, and he bears citation at some length on the point. He wanted to avoid war, 'but not at the expense either of our faith or honor.' He loved peace and was

... anxious that we should give the world still another useful lesson, by showing to them other modes of punishing injuries than by war, which is as much a punishment to the punisher as to the sufferer. I love, therefore, Mr. Clarke's proposition of cutting off all communications ... This, you will say, may bring on war. If it does, we will meet it like men; but it may not bring on war, & then the experiment will have been a happy one.[30]

Many points emerge in this statement. First, Jefferson retained at this stage the optimism of the eighteenth century that war could be eventually eliminated. Second, he placed much stress on the influence of man's reason in the conduct of affairs. Third, he believed that America could take a lead in showing how war might be banished from human affairs. Fourth, national honour was clearly important to Jefferson and he implied that war might be its only vindication. Fifth, Jefferson showed how important commerce had become in his mind if it might humble so mighty an antagonist as Great Britain. Finally, he did not see commercial interdiction as an ultimate weapon, since, if it failed, then war remained the final card Americans must play.

When the terms of Jay's Treaty became known in the United States, Jefferson believed it was a capitulation by the 'Anglomen' and 'Monocrats' who had gained an unnatural influence over George Washington. 'Acquiescence under insult is not the way to escape war.'[31] Political miscreants had opened the gates to tragedy, but however little Jay seemed to get for his country he had probably averted an Anglo-American war that would have been a disaster for the United States. Jefferson's partisanship blinded him to the Federalist accomplishment. The treaty came from peaceful negotiations and established a joint commission to arbitrate Anglo-American spoliation claims. As Lawrence Kaplan noted: 'Here was a clear cut victory of the principle of arbitration over the Old World principle of violence.'[32] Jefferson should have been jubilant. That he was not suggests how much he was in the grip of partisan suspicion.

When Jefferson returned to government as vice-president in 1796 a potential war with France threatened the tranquillity of America's existence. The Directory, angered because it considered Jay's Treaty a virtual Anglo-American alliance, and convinced that it could bully the United States into an attitude of hostility towards England, attempted to coerce America through decrees and privateers which caused serious losses to Yankee commerce. President John Adams retaliated with a request for a limited war of defence against French depredations. Jefferson hoped that Adams would be able to avert an open clash which would ruin American agriculture, commerce, and credit. For nearly three years, Franco-American relations would teeter on the brink of war, neither side wanting full belligerency, yet both sides sufficiently piqued to maintain a state of limited warfare waged sporadically at sea and by administrative decrees. During the Quasi-War, Washington's farewell advice to build a navy so that the United States could 'choose peace or war,' as their 'interest, guided by justice, shall counsel' seemed sound indeed.[33]

The conflict with France had many of the characteristics of war, but little real violence. No armies clashed. Little destruction resulted. The major losses for both sides lay in ships and sailors. The United States had a *de facto* ally in the British, who helped American vessels arm, provided the American government with materials of war, and permitted American merchantmen to sail with British convoys. But no formal alliance was declared with Britain, just as no formal war was declared against the French. Despite the machinations of a strident faction of the Federalist party and an orgy of indignation flowing from the revelations of the XYZ affair, popular opinion never wanted full-scale war. And John Adams, however much he favoured full belligerency with France, evaded a declared war through adroit diplomacy.

Jefferson believed at first that Adams was sincerely interested in avoiding war with France, but after a brief display of cordiality the two old friends drifted apart on rival political currents. Jefferson thought Adams fell under the influence of the 'Anglomen' who wanted to drag the United States into a war with its best friend against the wishes and interests of both countries. At this point Jefferson still thought of France as a potential counterpoise to British domination. But even this rational notion of balance became distorted by the violent partisanship of the time as Jefferson began to interpret national interests largely from his own perspective.[34]

Jefferson believed that the crisis would not have arisen had the United States been firm and just in its neutrality from 1793. He believed that those who had urged the necessity of the British connection were deluded at best and traitors at worst. They had caused the difficulty. True independence was impossible as long as the English continued to smother American commerce and finance. The Federalist press had an unwholesome and unnatural power, in his view, and it preached the heresy of an Anglo-American war against France. Some apostates had even gone so far as to suggest breaking up the union.[35] A conspiracy for war had grasped American policy. The bellicosity of the Federalists did not reflect the true views of Americans. Jefferson denied that military preparations would expedite negotiations, which was an interesting contrast to his suggestions in the 1780s rendered understandable only by his partisanship. He hoped that now a moderate opinion would grow in numbers and swell to a chorus of opposition.[36] Jefferson hammered at these themes in his correspondence throughout the summer of 1797 as he urged his friends to deflect the Federalist policies.

Jefferson's mood was mercurial. By June he was convinced that Adams's pacific professions were camouflage for warmongering behind the scenes. This threatened the very security of the United States since Louisiana could fall into French hands. Only the bad temper of two executives had brought two nations who loved each other to the brink of mutual carnage.[37] He was cheered to learn that Elbridge Gerry would form part of a new peace mission. Jefferson respected Gerry and wrote that peace was the first object, and, while 'interest & honor are also national considerations,' these favoured peace, not war. And hostilities could not erase past injuries. Besides, there was great danger that war would split the country, something Jefferson saw as a disaster.[38]

Jefferson then brought up commercial retaliation. Adams and Hamilton had rejected such a course with France, but Jefferson thought about the future, and in general rather than specific terms: 'War is not the best engine for us to resort to, nature has given us one *in our commerce*, which, if properly managed, will be a better instrument for obliging the interested nations of Europe to treat us with justice.'[39] If Americans had adopted such a policy in 1793 they would be standing on 'such an eminence of safety & respect as ages can never recover.' But the chance had been lost. Now the object was to salvage as much as possible. Once peace was restored in Europe, Jefferson believed that commercial relations between America and other nations should be so founded that justice would be their 'mechanical result.' Americans must make 'the interest of every nation stand surety for it's justice, & their own loss to follow injury to us ...'[40] This was all very well, but at no point did Jefferson indicate how this would affect Franco-American relations in 1797. He could only hope that events would work out favourably. Then, when the present smoke had cleared, America could wield her commercial bludgeon, 'provided we shall be willing to submit to occasional sacrifices, which will be nothing in comparison to the calamities of war.'[41]

Jefferson was wrenched back from musings about the future by the realities of the Franco-American march to war in 1797 and 1798. The Federalists became evil incarnate and he could not see the schisms beneath the surface which would lead to the defeat of the party in the election of 1800. The only dichotomy apparent to the vice-president was between those shrieking for war and those pleading for peace. The loudest warmongers were the 'Anglomen' who chased the British lion to satisfy their own ambition and greed, willing to suffer occasional scratches and bruises in exchange for power and wealth. The friends of peace had a hard struggle ahead in Jefferson's view, given the current political climate.[42]

The XYZ affair threatened to turn the march to war into a charge. Jefferson thought war and peace depended on a 'toss of cross and pile.' Even the Quakers refused to support a petition against war with France. He concluded that they were more attached to England than to either their principles or their own country. When the XYZ papers finally exploded into public news, Jefferson and the Republicans began to despair. All the champions of peace could do was 'attempt to prevent war measures *externally*, consenting to every rational measure of *internal* defence & preparation.' He noted that an act to allow the capture of French privateers was 'pretty generally considered as a commencement of war without a declaration,' and that members of Congress considered war as 'no longer doubtful.'[43] Jefferson thought that Adams had duped the people into believing that limited war measures would keep the peace. Only time would tell, of course, but French émigrés who had taken up residence in the United States did not wait. They began to move in anticipation of full-scale war.

Jefferson's best hope was European politics. He knew that international relations were unpredictable and time could work in America's favour. A French invasion of England, which seemed likely in 1798, could well smother the talk of war being broadcast by the 'Anglomen.' Time would also allow Americans to learn that the Federalists had been distorting the truth for their own selfish ends. Jefferson counselled delay because 'if we could but gain this season, we should be saved. The affairs of Europe would of themselves relieve us.'[44] In the event, he was right. The war-Federalists capitalized on popular outrage during the XYZ crisis but did not command sufficient strength to force their war, even in that heady summer of 1798. Jefferson was wrong when he thought that Adams was not working for peace and he was wrong when he smeared all Federalists with the same epithets, but he knew the fibres of American opinion when he stated that 'war, land & stamp tax are sedatives which must calm,' as Fries's Rebellion in western Pennsylvania revealed.[45] Although his view was intensely partisan, it had insight. In the election of 1800 the immense costs of the Federalists' war programme were vulnerable chinks in their political armour. Both Jefferson and Adams were peace candidates and their popular support suggests that the majority of Americans had not wanted war.

Jefferson's opposition to a Franco-American war was more than politically and emotionally inspired. Apart from repulsion at the prospect of human slaughter, he believed that American commerce, agriculture, independence, unity, and finance would suffer. He shuddered at the thought of his fellow citizens mortgaging their future income to debts created by war. America might well get to the bottom of her purse just in preparation. An empty treasury would be a poor deterrent, since bankruptcy was no condition in which to combat the greatest power on earth. Still, Jefferson would have accepted war if an attack had taken place. 'If our house be on fire, without inquiring whether it was fired from within or without, we must try to extinguish it.'[46]

The prospect of the Franco-American war seemed to upset what Jefferson saw as a necessary balance of the Constitution. Americans had placed the war power in Congress, in keeping with the eighteenth-century republican belief that executives were dangerously prone to war for frivolous reasons. In March of 1798 Jefferson hoped that an adjournment of Congress might take place, so that the people could be consulted by their representatives.[47] He noted to James Madison that Americans relied heavily on legislative control of war. The Federalists had evaded this by using a bare majority to push through military legislation which Jefferson feared would lead to war without the requisite consent of the people. Madison agreed: 'For if the opinion of the P[resident] not the facts & proofs themselves are to sway the judgement of Congress, in declaring war ... it is evident that the people are cheated out of the best ingredients in their Govt, the safeguards of peace ...'[48] But both men seemed oblivious both of Adams's efforts and of the fact that the Franco-American conflict had been closely controlled in law, in the best tradition of restraint in war which Jefferson championed.

By 1799 Jefferson was convinced that only Republican electoral success could effectively counter war.[49] He had become a thorough partisan and this coloured his view of foreign affairs in general just as it coloured his view of Franco-American difficulties. Jefferson explained himself in a lengthy letter to Elbridge Gerry, which seemed more like a campaign platform than a piece of private correspondence. He was against debt and a standing army, favoured a militia as a defensive force, and now looked askance on a navy, 'which, by its own expenses and the eternal wars in which it will implicate us, [will] grind us with public burthen, & sink us under them.' He was flatly against European entanglements and favoured free commerce. The war fever over France had always been artificial and had arisen because the people had not known the truth. After all, 'their sweat' would 'earn all the expences of the war, and their blood' would 'flow in extirpation of the causes of it.'[50] It was a succinct essay on a republican's view of war.

Jefferson maintained that the war crisis had been manufactured. The 'XYZ dish' had been 'cooked up by [John] Marshall, where the swindlers are made to appear as the French government.' News of peace from The Hague had at last caused the frenzy to flag. The people now knew that France had 'sincerely wished peace' and that the seducers of America had '... wished war, as well for the loaves & fishes which arise out of war expences, as for the chance of changing the constitution, while the people should have time to contemplate nothing but the levies of men and money.'[51] The Alien and Sedition Acts seemed to Jefferson the first signs of the coming Federalist dictatorship. The Republican cause would have been reduced to rubble and over the surface would have been cemented monarchy, either peaceably or by force of arms through provoking resistance.[52] Jefferson never knew how closely his suspicions corresponded to the schemes of Hamilton, Timothy Pickering, and the other war-Federalists. One of their primary motives had been the extermination of their Republican pests.

Jefferson's French sympathies began to ebb by 1800. The coup d'état of 18 Brumaire, which brought Napoleon Bonaparte to power, shattered his faith in the French Revolution. America was clearly a republic on its own in a monarchical ocean. Jefferson's letter to Gerry stated that he did not intend to enter 'that field of slaughter to preserve their balance' or join any 'confederacy of kings to war against the principles of liberty.'[53] Europe was a fount of war and any hopes for liberty rested with the future success of an independent American experiment. If Jefferson's political isolationism became irreversible at any time, this was the moment. America was clearly on her own, but he did not jettison the idea that European politics might be played to America's advantage.

Commercial interdiction as a substitute for war remained in the back of his mind all through the Franco-American crisis. He overlooked the fact that commercial non-intercourse with France was probably of some impact in the French decision to seek peace in 1799, having England as the primary target for any economic action. Merrill Peterson has made bold to assert that had Jefferson been in power in 1797 he would have avoided all military measures, permitted no bluster, and assumed a posture of friendship with France while arguing commercial action against England.[54] Certainly Jefferson wanted to check the power of Britain in American affairs. Given his intense mistrust of large military establishments, and their immense costs, trade seemed the most obvious weapon America could wield. There is little doubt that Jefferson would have been more pliable with France than the crusty John Adams. He would not have countenanced a limited war against the French, but in the face of an overt attack there is no reason to suppose he would not have made

a response in kind. Jefferson's sympathies for France, like his pacific disposition, had strict boundaries marked by danger to the American republic. Finally, Jefferson's optimism about the probable success of commercial action
lay over an underlying pessimism about human nature.

In truth, I do not recollect in all the animal kingdom a single species but man which is
eternally & systematically engaged in the destruction of its own species. What is called
civilization seems to have no other effect on him than to teach him to pursue the principle of *bellum omnium in omnia* on a larger scale, & in place of the little contests of tribe
against tribe, to engage all the quarters of the earth in the same work of destruction.[55]

Such a deep pessimism implies that however much he valued commercial interdiction Jefferson probably did not see it as an absolute solution to international disputes. Violence still lay behind whatever rational measures men
might employ.

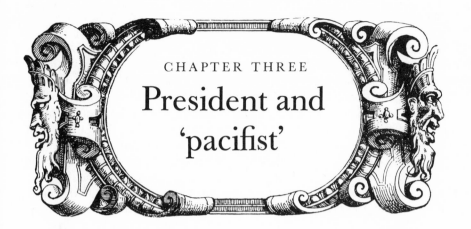

CHAPTER THREE

President and 'pacifist'

The lamentable resource of war is not authorized for evils of imagination, but for those actual injuries only, which would be more destructive of our well-being than war itself. JEFFERSON

The love of peace which we sincerely feel and profess, has begun to produce an opinion in Europe that our government is entirely in Quaker principles, and will turn the left cheek when the right has been smitten. This opinion must be corrected when just occasion arises, or we shall become the plunder of all nations. JEFFERSON[1]

War transformed the bright promise of the dawn of Jefferson's first presidency into the dim and disappointing twilight of the close of his second. Jefferson had little time to reflect on war during his eight years in office, because he was absorbed in the daily excitement and tedium of government. He maintained firm control over domestic politics, but in foreign affairs he held the initiative only fleetingly, when at all, because of the pressures exerted on the United States by a world in conflict. England and France had scant regard for the rights of weak neutrals as they locked in total war. Jefferson remained a man of the eighteenth century and did not realize that the age of limited conflicts had expired. Napoleon threw aside all restraints as he harnessed the energies of the Revolution in France to bid for world mastery.[2] The mental spectacles with which Jefferson viewed this contest were out of date. He still conceived of war as a dispute between governments.

One of Jefferson's first interests was economy in government. Albert Gallatin, Jefferson's secretary of the treasury, found much of his time involved with paring expenditures and the military was an obvious target. In his first annual message, Jefferson stated that 'sound principles' would not justify taxing

Americans to accumulate a war chest that might in itself constitute a temptation to war. In his second inaugural, he noted that, should war occur, increased revenues would allow its expenses to be met 'without encroaching on the rights of the future generations by burthening them with the debts of the past.'[3] He also feared the totalitarian tendencies inherent in war which would scuttle the Constitution which he saw as a 'peace establishment.'[4] As president, Jefferson sought to implement many of his conclusions about war.

Jefferson's interest in economy did not cause him to abandon all defensive preparations. He knew that national injuries would occasionally occur. Some could be healed amicably, but others were 'of a nature to be met by force only, and all of them may lead to it.' Although he was prepared to rely upon the power of American idealism to rally citizens when needed, he could not 'but recommend such preparations as circumstances call for.'[5] He therefore authorized the creation of the military academy at West Point and engaged in a more active defence programme after 1805 which emphasized fortifications and gunboats rather than militia. But all this did little to ready the country for any real war. The gunboats in particular have been much maligned, but, while their military value was negligible, they made sense in terms of Jefferson's largely defensive mentality and his policy of parsimony. His scheme for building a gargantuan dry dock to house frigates not in use reflected similar thinking. He believed this would 'save us great annual expence, & be an encouragement to prepare in peace the vessels we shall need in war ...'[6] Nothing came of the dry dock although several gunboats were built.

True to the Enlightenment, Jefferson placed great stress on reason as a deterrence: 'My hope of preserving peace for our country is not founded on the greater principles of non-resistance under every wrong, but in the belief that a just and friendly conduct on our part will procure justice and friendship from others.'[7] Taken by itself, such a view seems tragically naïve, but Jefferson coupled it with an opportunistic foreign policy. He was never prepared to prostrate his country in the face of aggression, although he would engage in extensive diplomatic writhing before admitting the necessity for force. He wrote during the embargo that the country had borne its wrongs stoically because 'if nations go to war for every degree of injury, there would never be peace on earth.' But he added that there was a time when resistance became 'morality.'[8] He knew that reason and justice could only provide partial bulwarks for his country.

Jefferson hoped to maintain a strict neutrality, as his first inaugural address, with its emphasis on 'peace, commerce, and honest friendship with all nations, entangling alliances with none,' revealed. Privately he wrote that to enter European conflicts 'would be to divert our energies from creation to destruction.'[9] To the ageing radical, Thomas Paine, he stated: 'Determined as we are to avoid, if possible, wasting the energies of our people in war and destruction, we shall avoid implicating ourselves with the powers of Europe, even in support of principles we mean to pursue. They have so many interests different from ours that we must avoid being entangled in them.'[10]

After the Peace of Amiens dissolved in May of 1803 Jefferson thought that Americans should observe the 'battle of lions & tygers' with 'no partialities.' By now he had completely abandoned any attachment to France, although his political enemies insisted that he was a fanatical 'jacobin.'[11] The weapon of 'passive coercion' was in the forefront of Jefferson's mind as a buttress for his neutrality.[12] He wanted to lighten the impact of war on mankind and argued for strict definition of contraband goods to try and avoid international incidents among belligerent powers. He was never able to accept British views on impressment and neutrals' rights, however, and learned quickly that in a world at war, the belligerents defined those rights.[13] Still, Jefferson's diplomacy ran along a clear line of development which was related to the outlines suggested by Vattel and others. The president sought to exploit every phase between peace and war to avoid open conflict, but was prepared to resort to force if pacific methods failed.[14]

Although Jefferson wanted to establish principles of justice and morality in international affairs, the imperatives of integrity, neutrality, and survival pushed this desire to second place much of the time. Jefferson's dream of an empire of republican liberty would vanish if America succumbed to the pressure of the European belligerents. He knew that Americans would rally to the flag if their homeland were in peril, but he also knew that occasions arose in international politics when a country must stand ready to fight, even though no direct menace had come into view. Also, he wanted to respect the war prerogatives of Congress.[15] He thus confronted the central dilemma of all conscientious democrats in power – how to balance executive initiatives with popular sanction. A president who refused to consult the people's representatives would be little better than the European monarchs Jefferson and his colleagues excoriated so frequently. On the other hand, Jefferson proved his own chief diplomat, using special agents in moments of crisis to supplement the customary channels of diplomatic communication. His approach to foreign policy therefore seems equivocal at times, and the great democrat occasionally resembled a paternal despot, wielding war and peace as instruments of his policy, convinced of the righteousness and wisdom of his own perspective.

Jefferson knew that America's independence rested to a great extent upon a balance of power in Europe.[16] He worked hard to stay out of European politics, but engaged in a limited war of his own against Tripoli. He profited from the war in Europe through the vast Louisiana concession from France. And he rattled his sabre continuously at Spain over the Floridas. Tripoli received his attention first, in the spring of 1801, when the pasha alleged that the Americans had insulted him by paying more tribute to Algiers. He promptly declared war on the United States in his time-honoured fashion by having the flagpole in front of the American consulate felled. After a brief and futile effort to settle the dispute, the consul departed and Jefferson decided to wage war, a policy he had always favoured.

The Tripolitan war was conducted with uneven enthusiasm and results by the United States, although the pasha was eventually forced to terms when a sizeable American fleet of thirty vessels assembled to blockade the harbour of Tripoli and bombard the city. Jefferson relied upon Congress to authorize him to conduct offensive operations, although his powers as commander-in-chief were probably sufficient. The legislature responded quickly by passing acts which allowed American warships to 'subdue, Seize, & make prize of all Vessels, goods, & effects, belonging to the Bey of Tripoli ...'[17] The war limped along, buoyed by a special Mediterranean fund devised by Gallatin, occasionally heroic naval exploits, and Jefferson's belief that the use of violence was a lesser evil than acceding to Barbary blackmail.[18]

Some contradictory currents ran beneath the surface of Jefferson's policy. He arranged for tribute to be sent to Algiers, even though he considered it 'money thrown away.' He resurrected the idea of a perpetual Mediterranean cruise by a concert of powers, and indeed there was some co-operation between American and other vessels, but he lamely stated that the legislature would perforce decide on the matter. It did not, and Jefferson does not seem to have pressed the issue with any vigour. He suggested to James Madison, his secretary of state, that he wanted to keep Algiers and Morocco 'friendly by a steady course of justice aided occasionally with liberality.' It later took a naval squadron to maintain the peace with Morocco. Actually, the other Barbary states were waiting to see how the United States fared with Tripoli. They were teetering on the brink of belligerency, and Jefferson did not want more than one war at a time, even against the African corsairs. In 1805 he admitted that his policy of limited war had not worked out well and that he would call all save a small blockading squadron home if peace did not ensue shortly. A blockade would cost little, since a few ships had to be maintained at sea anyway, and it would save the United States from 'increased tributes, and the disgrace attached to them.'[19] But the policy was finally successful. The peace with Tripoli stipulated ransom for prisoners, but no tribute. Jefferson's inconsistency stemmed from a desire to keep costs down and in balance with American pride. In sum, he had waged a limited war of policy much in the traditions of the eighteenth century, without violating his constitutional authority.

While the Tripolitan war spluttered, Jefferson was alarmed to learn that Louisiana had been retroceded to France by Spain in the Treaty of San Ildefonso in 1800. Rumours to this effect had been circulating for some time, and Jefferson realized, as he had before, that if a major power owned Louisiana American security was jeopardized. France would seek to exploit her possession with little regard for her neighbours. But Napoleon Bonaparte's preoccupation with Santo Domingo during the lull of Amiens prevented him from pursuing his dreams of a New World empire. This gave the United States a momentary reprieve, but when the Spanish intendant at New Orleans revoked the right of deposit guaranteed to the Americans by the Treaty of San Lorenzo of 1796, Jefferson had a potential war crisis on his hands.[20]

Westerners and Federalists clamoured for action and Jefferson made no effort to stifle their cries. But he did not intend to become involved in a war unless no other course lay open. He dispatched James Monroe to Paris to assist the regular minister, Robert Livingston, in negotiations to purchase New Orleans. At the same time he made military preparations.[21] The evidence suggests that he was even prepared to turn to Britain for help if bilateral diplomacy failed.[22] Jefferson had set the stage for such a threat a year before. In a lengthy letter to Livingston, which Jefferson had also shown to his informal agent, Pierre Samuel Dupont de Nemours, the president stressed that if France retained New Orleans she put herself in an 'attitude of defiance' towards the United States. Jefferson pleaded that he wanted to keep the peace, but it was out of his hands. Only France could avoid war by veering from her reckless course.[23] It is doubtful that such conventional histrionics made much impression on Napoleon, but Jefferson mounted the best bluster he could manage.

Henry Adams argued that Jefferson never intended to use force, since he clung to peace with an almost obsessive passion.[24] It is true that Jefferson wrote Livingston in October 1802 that 'no matter' was important enough 'to risk a breach of the peace.' But early the following year he wrote to Monroe that if the United States could not acquire peace through purchase, '... then as war cannot be distant, it behooves us immediately to be preparing for that course, without, however, hastening it, and it may be necessary (on your failure on the continent) to cross the channel.'[25] Jefferson was probably serious. He seemed to be preparing for every contingency, while stalling for time, until the debt could be discharged and American settlers could swarm into the Mississippi country. The president noted to W.C.C. Claiborne, the future governor of Louisiana, that war in Europe would make New Orleans easier to obtain, and although he hoped to avoid the use of force the region would be simple enough to seize.[26] War may have been a last resort for Jefferson, but it was always an alternative.

The multiple offensive proved unnecessary. Napoleon decided to sell all Louisiana, not just New Orleans, for reasons unrelated to American diplomacy. The imperial eagle of France thought the American eaglet scarcely worth a sneer, but American money was welcome. The vagaries of European politics had come to Jefferson's rescue. After a brief flurry of negotiating, where the only haggling was over price, the 'noble bargain' was struck. The astonished Americans found themselves the proud possessors of vast and vague Louisiana, not just New Orleans and a small stretch of riverbank.

Jefferson engaged in some modest self-congratulation over his triumph. He boasted that he had obtained by a 'reasonable and peaceable process' in just four months '... what would have cost us 7 years of war, 100,000 human lives, 100,000 millions of additional debt, besides ten hundred millions lost by the want of market for our produce, or depredations on it seeking markets, and the general demoralization of our citizens which war occasions.'[27] This was sheer speculative hyperbole since Jefferson had only snatched up an offer no sane statesman would have refused. But he showed determination when the Spanish appeared reluctant about turning Louisiana over to American control. He ordered an immediate reconnaissance to spy out what forces Spain had to defend the territory and how the inhabitants would respond to the arrival of American soldiers. Plans were laid to send regulars west, mobilize already organized militia from the Mississippi Territory, and call upon the governors of Kentucky and Tennessee for additional troops.[28] These martial preparations were unnecessary since on the appointed day the Spanish turned formal control of Louisiana over to the French, who shortly thereafter relinquished command to the Americans. The United States had acquired Louisiana without a military incident, as Jefferson had hoped, but he was always prepared to use force in defence of what he perceived as American vital interests.

Despite the ease with which Louisiana was acquired, Spanish-American relations continued to be stormy. By 1805 Jefferson was engaged in a campaign of persuasion, bribery, and threat to seize the Floridas. He had coveted them for some time and now he brandished spurious legal claims, based on old maps which inflated Louisiana's already vague boundaries, as though they were anointed titles. He offered to exchange the Floridas for old American spoliation claims dating to the Quasi-War. He spouted righteous wrath and seemed perpetually on the verge of unleashing his battalions, but he was not able to convince the Spanish he was serious. He responded quickly when the Spanish made incursions into American territory, noting in his annual message of 1805 that formal war was neither necessary nor probable, '... but the protection of our citizens, the spirit and honor of our country require that force should be interposed to a certain degree. It will probably continue to advance the object of peace.'[29] Early in 1806 Jefferson explained to Dupont de Nemours that the United States had restrained itself with Spain out of respect for France, which was real enough. He might well have been determined to 'take or obtain our just limits,' but he could do little while Spain was supported by the major belligerents in Europe. He had convinced himself none the less that the Floridas would be just indemnification for past wrongs, forgetting that national interests and natural rights were not synonymous.[30]

Jefferson was nothing if not persistent with the Spanish, despite his lack of success, and he made every effort to gain the initiative in Spanish-American relations. Distance from Europe and the swift pace of events there did not allow an opportunistic foreign policy to function effectively, so he experienced continual frustration. At the same time, he provided for blockhouses, gunboats, and militia supplies for the southwest. He even suggested a bounty scheme to attract able-bodied settlers who would form a defensive militia, but nothing came of this idea.[31] He argued that the suppression of Aaron Burr's plot to foment revolution in Spanish America was proof of his good faith with Spain, but by the summer of 1807, at the height of an Anglo-American crisis, he wanted the United States to make a 'remonstrance & demand satisfaction ...' If Congress approved, reprisals could be mounted. 'Our southern defensive force can take the Floridas, volunteers for a Mexican army will flock to our standard, and rich pabulum will be offered to our privateers in the plunder of their commerce & coasts. Probably Cuba would add itself to our confederation.'[32]

The president sounded as though he had scotched Burr's plans for an invasion so that they would not interfere with his own. He suggested to Madison that war should be avoided with every power except Spain. Even while he augmented forces because of the English threat he wanted troops ready to seize the Floridas if a good opportunity arose. In 1808 he argued that if England and the United States did not go to war, and if Spain became enmeshed with Napoleon, then it would be a good time to take reprisals on the Floridas for Spain's refusal to meet past demands. But Madison and Gallatin were both alarmed at such expansionism, and countered Jefferson's arguments, dampened his fires, and were generally effective in restraining the uncharacteristically warlike president.[33]

Jeffersons's belligerence towards Spain was an amalgam of several forces.

By 1807 and 1808 he experienced the strain of leadership in a world that seemed to be sliding deeper into chaos. He had convinced himself that American interests in Florida were rights bestowed by nature, and this heightened his sense of indignation. The Spanish were both obdurate and protected by powerful friends. All these points combined to create Jefferson's contempt for Spain and his bellicosity, which, for a republican president, was as real as that of any despotic monarch coveting his neighbour's territory. Jefferson's efforts to use war as policy to obtain the Floridas was a failure. He seemed like Louis XIV, wanting to round America's frontiers to their natural limits, as he defined them.

Spanish-American affairs faded in significance as English-American relations stumbled over the pressures created by the war in Europe. Napoleon broadened his campaign by embarking on an economic offensive with the Berlin decree of 21 November 1806. The English retaliated with the Orders-in-Council the following year. Napoleon declared that there could be no neutrals and sought to enlist either the passive or active support of the United States. Britain, on the other hand, could not permit the Americans to succour any enemy that would have seen her reduced to penury, impotence, and subjection. In such an atmosphere, the voices of reason shouted into the wind.

The European conflict provided the context for Jefferson's supreme effort to lessen the impact of war on mankind. Faced with expensive and humiliating losses of ships, property, and seamen, and the armed might of the most powerful military nations on earth, the president sensibly sought an alternative to war to shore up American neutrality and sovereignty. Jefferson turned to economic interdiction, although he vastly overestimated its power. More important, he did not understand the true nature of the war in Europe, the complexity of the Atlantic economy, the foundation of British politics, or the determination of England to defeat the tyrant Bonaparte. Great Britain saw herself as a dike of liberty against the tide of Napoleonic totalitarianism. This belief sapped the strength of Jefferson's weapon, but the president was also determined. Henry Adams may well have been correct when he wrote that Jefferson was so '... confident in his theory of peaceable coercion that he would hardly have thought his administration complete had he quitted office without being allowed to prove the value of his plan.'[34]

At first, Jefferson sought to redeem the situation by diplomacy. James Monroe went to London in 1806 to find accommodation on the apparently insoluble issues of impressment and continual seizures. Although he had seen as early as 1803 that the British would be stubborn over impressment, Jefferson never did understand that they could not discard the principal means of manning their navy.[35] In 1804 he noted that 'it will be necessary for us to

consider of a gradation of peaceable measures which may coerce the belligerent powers into an obedience to the laws within our waters' when English
press gangs operated in American ports and French privateers violated the
rules of neutrality. He mulled over quarantining the armed ships of offending
nations by denying them supplies, denying their trading vessels access to
American ports, '& lastly to recur to force.' He even suggested using the navy,
such as it was, to keep foreign privateers away.

When an American seaman was killed by a warning shot fired from the
British cruiser *Leander* outside New York, Jefferson translated his musings into
action. He banned the *Leander* and her two consorts from American harbours
and issued an order for the arrest of her captain.[36] This incident, in combination with general British arrogance and hostility, as manifested in English-
man James Stephen's influential pamphlet, *War in Disguise, or the Frauds of
Neutral Flags,* which excoriated Americans as tacit allies of Napoleon, led
Congress to pass the first Non-Importation Act in 1806. Jefferson held this in
abeyance as a sign of good faith to aid the negotiations in London, but the
British refused to be either mollified or intimidated. The English did request
that non-importation be banned by any new agreement, and Monroe, along
with William Pinkney, the American minister in Britain, concurred. They
understood the British position better than Jefferson and had a more realistic
assessment than their home government about what would be feasible in any
new Anglo-American arrangement.[37]

The Monroe-Pinkney negotiations wandered through a tortuous course
rendered more difficult by war passions, changes of government in England,
and an American president who rejected the final document out of hand. Jefferson complained that it said nothing about impressment and tied up his
hands by denying the United States the use of non-importation for ten years.
He did not want his favourite, albeit untried, weapon defused before it could
be brought into action. The president's behaviour was summary as well as
galling to the American representatives in London, because the power to re-
ject treaties supposedly lay with the Senate, and not the executive.[38] Jefferson
showed once more that he could be despotic in his own paternal way. Anglo-
American relations were, therefore, at an impasse, and Jefferson suggested
that the discussion might take a 'friendly nap' while something new was
worked out. By June of 1807, things were quiet, if unsettled, when lightning
struck.

On 22 June *H.M.S. Leopard* pounded the American frigate *Chesapeake* with
several broadsides when the British were refused the privilege of mustering
the American crew to search for deserters. When these were removed, and the
badly damaged *Chesapeake* limped back to Norfolk, Virginia, from which she

had left just that morning, Jefferson had an instantaneous war crisis on his hands. The country made a strident response and Jefferson commented he had never seen such unity since the Battle of Lexington. Anti-British riots flared in Norfolk, where water casks intended for the English war vessels were smashed. As the news spread, protests were mounted and newspapers from Massachusetts to Georgia screamed defiance. Even the Federalists joined hands with Republicans to chorus their rage. Militia units were mustered in Virginia and patrolled the shorelines, capturing a hapless English boat crew, which Jefferson ordered released as a token of good will. The president collected his cabinet, took what immediate measures he could in case the British planned further aggressions, and determined upon a course of action, but he did not call Congress.[39]

Jefferson refused to call the people's representatives for several reasons. Summer in Washington was the fever season, but, more important, he wanted time for tempers to cool, for the British government to disavow the action of the *Leopard's* commander, to make military preparations, and to allow American merchant ships to come home. Given the temper of the country, to call Congress would have meant he wanted war, and Jefferson worked to avoid it if he could. The *Revenge*, an armed vessel, was dispatched to London for a British explanation. All British armed vessels were ordered out of American ports and all intercourse with them was forbidden. Stephen Decatur, the naval officer commanding at Norfolk, was ordered to resist forcibly if any British warships tried to enter American rivers, although he was not to provoke an incident. By August, Jefferson had declared that all British armed vessels were to be treated as public enemies. English landing parties were liable to be killed or captured, and communications with the British ships could only take place under flag, as in time of war. More gunboats were ordered ready, the initial phases of militia mobilization were taken up, arrangements were made to strengthen existing fortifications and prepare new defensive works, war materials were collected, contracts for equipment were let, and tentative plans were even laid for invasion of parts of Canada. [40]

Jefferson took all the steps required by the then law of nations. He coupled diplomacy with quiet preparedness to await the fall when word could be expected from England and Congress would meet. Besides, whether the *Chesapeake-Leopard* affair was a 'proper cause of war' was for Congress to decide. Jefferson wanted to commit no act which might perforce be later retracted.[41] He moved to prevent further insults and '... leave Congress free to decide whether war is the most efficacious mode of redress in our case, or whether, having taught so many other useful lessons to Europe, we may not add that of showing them that there are peaceable means of repressing injustice ...'[42] Although he stated repeatedly that he would accept congressional guidance, by the summer of 1807 it was likely that Jefferson wanted to try his scheme of peaceful coercion if the British refused to give satisfaction.[43] Here was Jefferson the Enlightenment prophet of progress at his best. He was close to the climax of his career, a supreme effort to find a substitute for war.

Bradford Perkins believes that Jefferson sought to sustain the crisis. In June, Perkins suggests, Jefferson had war and did not want it; in October, he wanted war but did not have it.[44] Jefferson did stall for time. He wanted the English to know that they had committed a major wrong, and he wanted time for diplomacy and preparedness, but at no time did he want war, despite the fact that he was prepared to accept it if all else failed. Jefferson did not really expect justice from England, however, and he noted: 'A war need cost us very little; and we can take from them what would be an indemnification for a great deal. For this everything shall be in readiness the moment it is declared.'[45] Jefferson never did move the country into much of a state of readiness, but in his mind he was following a rational progression – diplomacy, passive coercion, limited reprisal, open war – in his effort to protect the United States.

Jefferson became firm to the point of truculence by October. American shipping continued to suffer from seizures and seamen continued to be impressed. The British betrayed no hint of yielding or remorse. It was the bludgeoning of the economic war in Europe, more than the *Chesapeake-Leopard* affair on its own, that prompted Jefferson to shift from diplomacy to passive coercion. Some form of retaliation was clearly in order, but war did not seem either practical or justified. On 31 December 1807 he requested an embargo on all American shipping as the only apparent alternative. The initial legislation, which Congress passed with almost indecent haste, was sketchy to an extreme, with little evidence of thought or planning behind it. Subsequent measures strengthened the embargo, and attempted to plug leaks which became evident with the passage of time, such as illegal trading into Canada.[46] The embargo was intended as a coercive measure from the beginning, and it came from an eighteenth-century mind which was optimistic enough to believe that man might find a substitute for war as a means of settling his disputes.

Jefferson did not necessarily see the embargo as an ultimate method of seeking redress for grievances. In March 1808 he took it to be 'an universal opinion that war will become preferable to a continuance of the embargo after a certain time.' He called the embargo the 'last card' Americans had to play 'short of war.' In May he stated: 'How long the continuance of the embargo may be preferable to war, is a question we shall have to meet, if the decrees & orders & war continues.' By June he asserted that the day was not distant when war would be preferable. 'But,' he added, 'we can never remove that, & let our vessels go out & be taken ... without making reprisal.'[47]

The president seems to have realized that the embargo was only an alternative to war if it led to a settlement. If the belligerents refused to be intimidated, then it was an intervening step between diplomatic remonstrance and open conflict, no more a solid alternative to war than either diplomacy or restricted reprisals. It was a limited measure, designed to apply pressure on the material self-interest of an antagonist. The embargo's major flaws were its foundation in a rational view of man's behaviour and Jefferson's failure to understand the complexity of the European war and Britain's economy. Economics and reason alone do not rule history. The British were fighting a crusade, and as crusaders they equated self-interest with victory and survival rather than simple profits. Neither the British nor the French would listen to the version of reason preached by the Americans. The embargo proved to be a step on the road to war, rather than its alternative.

Jefferson knew some of this when he called for the embargo, but he reasoned at first that the measure would gain time during which peace might emerge in Europe and American defences could be strengthened. He realized that America's peril stemmed from the European conflagration. But even by itself the embargo might succeed. Jefferson and the Republicans had advocated the use of economic coercion for nearly twenty years and the president placed 'immense value in the experiment being fully made, how far an embargo may be an effectual weapon in the future as well as on this occasion.'[48] In an experimental society, experimental weapons were perfectly logical. In time, Jefferson asserted that the embargo demonstrated American 'moderation and firmness' and had 'frustrated those usurpations and spoliations which, if resisted, involved war; if submitted to, sacrificed a vital principle of our national independence.'[49] Once again, Jefferson revealed the basic denominator in his approach to both foreign policy and war, the survival and security of his country.

The president looked to Congress to provide additional refinements to his embargo, and Republican majorities ensured their production. Despite raucous Federalist protests, the measure enjoyed widespread support throughout the United States. But enforcement proved a perpetual headache and Jefferson moved, albeit reluctantly, towards greater use of federal power in an effort to make his vessel watertight. As a result, the United States experienced some of the same despotic control that accompanies the advent of most wars. Although Jefferson appeared at his most tyrannical by enforcing the embargo, there is no reason to doubt that this caused him genuine agony. Some measure of a warlike atmosphere was evident in his tendency to speak of opposition as treasonous, but he continued to rely upon the will of the legislature to either continue or cast down the embargo.[50]

It was unfortunate that the president gave only passive leadership in a national effort that required the discipline of war but which lacked the stimulus to patriotic enthusiasm aroused by the prospect of the homeland in danger. William James once spoke of the need for a 'moral equivalent' for war which would evoke heroism, determination, discipline, and a sense of self-sacrifice without carnage and destruction. When he discussed the embargo as a substitute for war, Henry Adams wrote: 'If war made men brutal, at least it made them strong; it called out the qualities best fitted to survive in the struggle for existence. To risk life for one's country was no mean act ... War, with all its horrors, could purify as well as debase; it dealt with high motives and vast interests; taught courage, discipline, and stern sense of duty.'[51]

James and Adams reflected the perspective of a later age, but the point has a timeless quality. If Jefferson sought a true alternative to war, his insight failed to grasp the nature of the conflict that raged in Europe and the nature of the emotions that need to be aroused for a disciplined national enterprise. Jefferson was the product of an age where the psychological perspectives of James and Adams were impossible. The eighteenth century thought in terms of the rational and civilized control of war as an instrument of state policy, not of war as a crusade or moral purgative. Jefferson's rational response to the Napoleonic holocaust was, therefore, anachronistic. It reflected a noble sentiment and a princely ambition, but, given the circumstances, it could not succeed. It was based on an intellectual perspective out of phase with the currents of history. The French Revolution and Napoleon had rendered restraint in war obsolete.

A clue that Jefferson did not really connect his own image of war with reality emerged in a few comments he made about debt. Albert Gallatin pointed out in October 1808 that future revenues would be insufficient for either war or a continuation of the embargo. Yet Jefferson could write: 'we wish to avoid the necessity of going to war, till our revenue shall be entirely liberated from debt. Then it will suffice for war without creating new debt or taxes.' Early in 1809 he wrote: 'If we go to war now, I fear we may renounce forever the hope of seeing an end of our national debt. If we can keep peace eight years longer, our income, liberated from debt, will be adequate to any war ...'[52] Such a view was unrealistic, based more on dogma than rational analysis, although it suggested how closely he linked war and debt. In turn, this offers a clue for understanding his recommendation of such a policy, apart from its pacifist qualities. He was balancing projected costs and gains. But the embargo had prostrated American exports, trade, and the customs receipts.

By late 1808 the losses from the embargo exceeded the potential losses of war, as Jefferson came to see just before he left office. In March 1809 he wrote that the embargo had been removed 'because 50 millions of exports, annually sacrificed, are treble of what war would cost us. Besides that by war we shall take something, & lose less than at present.'[53] Jefferson's pacifism apparently had strict limits, marked out in part by negative balances in the nation's ledgers. He was reluctant to 'take the tented field' again, but he was prepared to fight rather than submit, even though by 1809 it was unclear whether England or France was the enemy in view of Napoleon's ravaging of American vessels.[54] Jefferson left office believing that only a short time more would have produced the results he anticipated, but that seems doubtful. Despite higher prices and opposition in Britain, the circumstances were unfavourable and the British had a discipline and determination bred of war that the Americans seemed to lack.

Historians have roughly agreed that the embargo was an instrument of coercion with precautionary and procrastinative overtones, and they have agreed that it failed, despite its mixed impact both at home and abroad. But beyond that there has been a lack of consensus, particularly in the view of Jefferson. Henry Adams saw the embargo as an outgrowth of Republican theory, Jefferson's opportunism, and the president's fear that war would scuttle the American experiment. Louis Sears, in a conscious effort to counter Adams's cynicism, saw Jefferson as a pacifist attempting to put his theories into practice. Bradford Perkins believed that Jefferson badly miscalculated, even bungled, and produced a mere 'sketch of policy' which was not thought through and which spasmodically evolved into a semi-permanent institution. Leonard Levy pictured Jefferson as a confused, frustrated man, a virtual apostate and tyrant making war on his own people to prevent a war against the Europeans. Merrill Peterson argued that the embargo was a logical development of Jeffersonianism, and an effort to prove the virtues of republican America. Dumas Malone advanced a thesis close to Perkins's, albeit softer, and saw Jefferson deliberately select a policy of procrastination to avoid an unwise war which would have meant an abdication of neutrality, and hence a loss of independence.[55]

All of these perspectives have merit and insight, but any attempt to evaluate the embargo as an alternative to war must start with its failure. Prices were driven up in England, the West Indies did experience privation, and havoc did strike manufacturers in Britain dependent upon the American export market. But Britons tightened their belts, substitute markets emerged in South America, and those elements which suffered the most were politically impotent. The parliamentary opposition was weak and easily discredited. Finally, the British were convinced that the Americans suffered more than they did. As Bradford Perkins noted, the embargo had visited all the privations of war upon the United States, but with none of the compensations.[56] Napoleon even welcomed the embargo as a tacit compliance with his Continental System. As a result, it had no effect on the European edicts. In time, the British did prove willing to withdraw the Orders-in-Council, but this was after a severe depression and at a time when Napoleon seemed more dangerous than ever. The international world was too complex and unpredictable for an instrument like Jefferson's embargo to have the coercive effect intended. War proved necessary after all to show American independence and determination, although it did not come for three more years.

After a confused debate through the winter of 1808-9, where Jefferson virtually abdicated leadership and Congress seemed paralyzed, the embargo was replaced with commercial non-intercourse. Jefferson signed the Non-Intercourse Act on 4 March 1809, the day he left office. The embargo had failed and created a storm of controversy in the country which left a dark pall over Jefferson as he headed into permanent retirement.

Jefferson had continued military preparations through the period of the embargo, although he scarcely turned America into a state where it would have been ready for war. Congress was reluctant to vote funds, but Jefferson had always known that if peaceable coercion failed more forceful measures would inevitably be needed to avoid submission if the European belligerents did not rescind their edicts. He was bitter over the opposition that had arisen to the embargo because he believed it only encouraged Britain and France to remain stubborn. He suggested in January 1809 that Congress might still want to stop short of war by issuing letters of marque and reprisal. 'This will let Europe see that our purpose is war without expressing it authoritatively.'[57] Such a suggestion contradicted his intense criticism of John Adams's limited reprisals against France in 1797 and 1798. But Jefferson was like so many men who have viewed the exercise of power from both sides of the fence. Criticism is easier when not actually in control, and contradictions are not noticed because individuals are so often convinced that their own perceptions represent reality while those of their opponents are malicious or simply stupid. Finally, Jefferson had always been convinced that England was the enemy and he conducted his policies with that premise in mind.

At the very end Jefferson resurrected an old scapegoat for war. He scorned that 'protruberant navigation' which had kept the United States in 'hot water' since 1789. An 'exuberant commerce' was now dragging the country into war. It would bring Americans 'into collision with other powers in every sea,' and would force them into 'every war of the European powers.'[58] This was only partly true. The Napoleonic Wars, not American commerce, had created the difficulties. In time of peace, American trade could compete quietly, subject to only occasional strictures. But the dangers of commerce had been a persistent theme in Jefferson's thought since his 'Notes on the State of Virginia,' even though the current outburst reflected the frustration of a disappointed man whose fondest hopes had been dashed and who had probably been too long in office.

The most enlightened thought on war and peace in the eighteenth century, along with American experience and Republican doctrine, formed the background for the embargo. It had failed because it was anachronistic and because it was posited in the belief that men would respond rationally to protect their self-interest, which Jefferson saw largely in material terms. Europe was engaged in total war where self-interest was ambition, and power, not reason, was the telling argument.

CHAPTER FOUR

Sage and nationalist

O Brother, if we were to escape from this war and be ageless and deathless forever, never would I send thee into men-enobling battles. But now, since unnumbered deadly fates stand about us which men may not avoid let us go forward. HOMER

I hope it is practicable, by improving the mind and morals of society, to lessen the disposition to war; but of its abolition I despair. JEFFERSON[1]

In March 1809, when he left Washington and headed south to Monticello, Thomas Jefferson made two journeys at once – a physical trek and a symbolic pilgrimage from first citizen of the Republic to retired sage. Retirement scarcely meant seclusion, despite the pall cast by the embargo and the unresolved crisis with England. Jefferson was on public display at Monticello, and he basked in the admiring light of a host of visitors and correspondents. Even out of harness he could not devote as much time as he had hoped to his books, farming, family, and plans for education. His wrist stiffened from age and old injury, yet he struggled to answer a constant stream of letters. He viewed each one he received as a miniature debt of honour, and bemoaned his fate as a correspondent, but one suspects it was a sweet pain he endured on the rack of his writing table. His letters were rich, and revealed a broad, inquiring, learned, and lucid mind which was capable of covering myriad subjects with ease and felicity. Jefferson showed himself to be an encyclopaedist by nature if not by trade.

His view of war again emerged largely through his reaction to events. He remained in close touch with national affairs through the pipelines of the *Richmond Enquirer*, the Philadelphia *Aurora*, the *National Intelligencer*, and the letters and visits of his friends and acquaintances. The major officers of the government, present and future, freely consulted his advice from time to time and in the process kept him abreast of the problems of his country.[2]

While Congress and James Madison's administration played variations on the theme of economic coercion, Jefferson continued to defend his choice of an embargo. He believed that the United States would have compelled England to come to terms 'by peaceable means, and the embargo, evaded as it was, proved it would have coerced her had it been honestly executed.'[3] But the war in Europe and Federalist treason had eroded the embargo. At any other time, such a measure would have been effective, 'but the hurricane which is now blasting the world, physical and moral, has prostrated all the mounds of reason as well as right.' At last Jefferson began to gain some insight into the failure of his beloved weapon. He had always known that the struggle of the European titans imperilled his country's independence and well-being, but he had placed too much faith in the embargo to protect America from an armed world and help her avoid the 'desolating calamities inseparable from war ... and the dangers it threatens to free governments ...'[4] He still did not realize how much his efforts to enforce the embargo had brought both of those woes to his fellow citizens.

Jefferson thought that if Britain's attacks on trade continued war would become almost inevitable. 'Our misunderstandings with England now seem to have reached their ne plus ultra,' he wrote, 'and it is difficult to see what will be the next move. [I]f not war, it may be the immediate Generator of War.'[5] Jefferson predicted hostilities for as early as May 1809 if the British and French edicts remained in force. He wrote to Madison that America would have 'credit with the world' if it could avoid the European vortex, but war could become a 'less losing business than unresisted depredation.' Before a recourse to violence, however, Jefferson favoured one further attempt at peaceful coercion by denying the offenders American commercial carrying services.[6] Given the fate of the embargo, it is difficult to see what this would have accomplished.

Jefferson's apprehension that English arrogance would goad America into war heightened as 1812 approached. He brightened momentarily at news of the ill-fated Erskine Agreement of April 1809, which seemed to offer an accommodation, and wrote Madison that it represented a 'triumph of our forbearing and yet persevering system.' But Britain rejected the agreement, and rebuked its representative for exceeding his instructions. Jefferson became depressed. England would not compromise, and if Napoleon had the sense to correct himself war with England was probably inescapable.[7] He accepted at face value, as did Madison, the French emperor's bogus withdrawal of his edicts, and stated that one power had got out of America's way and left her a clear field with the other. In light of the terms of Macon's Bill no. 2, he seemed correct, but this was just what Napoleon wanted the Americans to think.

Jefferson's Anglophobia ebbed and flooded from time to time, but it never completely abated. He was convinced in 1811 that England was infected with a national disease which drove her to seek a monopoly of world trade by crushing all competition. He did not believe she actively desired war with the United States, but thought her ministers were prepared to accept this rather than abandon the chance for maritime ascendancy. Jefferson was close to the end of his tether. 'We have hitherto been able to avoid professed war ... But the determination to take all our vessels bound to any other than her ports, amounting to all the war she can make (for we fear no invasion), it would be folly in us to let that war be all on one side only, and to make no effort towards indemnification and retaliation by reprisal.'[8]

The United States could both gain and lose in a new war with England in Jefferson's view. First, there was the question of preparedness, and, although Jefferson believed this was adequate for defence, the war divulged that the country was pitifully vulnerable to attack, if not conquest. He and the Republicans placed unwarranted faith in the militia myth, expecting the people to convert to a 'nation of warriors' virtually overnight. But territorial rewards beckoned, and American weaknesses were not apparent. Jefferson thought that the Georgia militia alone could seize the Floridas in a matter of weeks. The sage cast his gaze to the north as well, and talked in terms once again reminiscent of Louis xiv's compulsion to expand France to her natural frontiers.[9]

Jefferson also knew that severe risks would march in the train of war. The Federalists could refuse to defend the realm; perhaps they would even make a separate peace with England and split the union. This was no idle fancy, as the war revealed. Jefferson wanted to publicize the benefits of union and use the wars of Europe to illustrate the 'abject depression and degredation' which could arise. And there was a question of money: 'I consider the fortunes of our republic as depending ... on the extinguishment of the public debt before we engage in any war: because that done we shall have revenue enough to improve our country in peace and defend it in war without recurring either to new taxes or loans.'[10] He was certain that the president would pursue peace with the belligerents until it became 'more losing than war' and that the 'total extinction of the national debt, & liberation of our revenue' would cause the country tb bless Madison's retirement.[11] But peace was elusive, and war eventually added the burdens Jefferson feared so much to the demands on the public treasury.

The ex-president expressed reservations about the competence of Congress to manage a war effort because of the 'lying and licentious character of our papers' and the 'wonderful credulity of the members of Congress in the floating lies of the day.' Besides, he doubted the efficiency of any body containing nearly one hundred lawyers. Finally, he cautioned that war made the people look to the executive, not the legislature.[12] Belligerency could undermine democracy itself. These were puzzling comments coming from a lawyer who had been dictatorial at times in his relationships with Congress while president, but who had customarily been highly solicitous of congressional views and sensibilities, not to mention popular opinion. Perhaps Jefferson's years in office had lowered his esteem of the legislature, and perhaps his own convictions had caused him to lose some perspective on himself at the same time.

Despite the plethora of uncertainties Jefferson readily accepted the War of 1812 when it arrived. Impressment and the Orders-in-Council acquitted the United States of any taint of aggression and rendered war 'no longer avoidable.' The English effort to control the oceans meant battle with the world, until she fell enervated and bankrupt. 'Every hope from time, patience, and the love of peace is exhausted, and war or abject submission are the only alternative left us.' The debt would remain and America would become a nation of soldiers, but capitulation without a struggle was unthinkable to the nationalistic Jefferson. He once wrote that the 'laws of necessity, of self-preservation, of saving our country when in danger' were transcendent considerations. Faced with starvation of its soul, the nation could seize sustenance by violence.[13]

If there was ever a reluctant belligerent, it was the United States in 1812. Jefferson's personal hopes and fears about the results of war were mirrored in the debate and close voting in Congress. But Jefferson also reflected the sense of wounded national honour which lay at the core of the American decision in 1812. Even as Congress discussed Madison's request for a war vote, Jefferson took passage for granted and prayed it would '... end in indemnity for the past, security for the future, and compleat emancipation from Anglomany, Gallomany, and all the manias of demoralized Europe ...'[14] Jefferson's isolationism was running strongly. When news of the vote arrived, he noted that it was well received in Virginia. The war was just because the only alternative had been 'abandonment of the persons and property of our citizens on the ocean,' which no American could tolerate.[15] And Britain was the enemy, despite French depredations. Discussion had arisen about a possible 'triangular war' against both European powers, but this madness was quickly discarded. Jefferson objected on the practical grounds that American privateers, upon which he placed great reliance, would have no friendly ports in which to dispose of their prizes.[16]

Although the war as voted was unrestricted, it had important characteristics which placed it firmly in the traditions of the age of limited war. Despite grandiose proclamations, the Americans invaded Canada and attacked British shipping for the same reason – to apply pressure for accommodation over impressment, and later to have the Indians restrained, once it was learned that the Orders-in-Council had been withdrawn. The United States was using armed force as a method of arbitration to achieve satisfaction for specific injuries received. The war was not waged for conquest, despite a crusading rhetoric.

Jefferson generated considerable militant enthusiasm, but his eighteenth-century sense of restraint was really in command. Before the war he had noted that enemies could trade during hostilities, provided this was 'mutually advantageous to the individuals, and not to their injury as belligerents.' He saw no reason why certain trade should not continue with the English during the war itself, as it did for a time with Arthur Wellesley's army in the Iberian peninsula. In 1813 Jefferson argued that the Americans could scarcely hope to starve England by refusing to sell her grain. After all, other suppliers would only step into the breach. It was not reasonable to expect Americans to relinquish a profit when it would make no difference to the war effort.[17] But Jefferson was disarmingly candid and even slightly sophistical when he asserted that Britain was really doing the United States a favour by keeping certain continental ports out of Napoleon's clutches. Therefore, trade should not be denied. The sage of Monticello was more cunning than his apparently guileless desire for profit would suggest. He was convinced that if markets remained open his countrymen would support the American war effort with less reluctance. They would be able to sell their produce and the customs revenues would help to offset the expenses of the fighting.[18] Jefferson wanted the advantages of both war and peace in the Anglo-American conflict.

Such an attitude is little short of astounding to a mind conditioned by the experience of the wars of the twentieth century, where all communications between enemies are severed, and where virtue and evil take on tribal associations. War is much more complex than the simple notion of an 'enemy' would imply, however, and in the eighteenth century Jefferson's view was perfectly logical. War was an affair between governments, and Jefferson often drew a distinction between the English people and their régime. America mustered her forces against the monarch and his ministry. When Anglo-American belligerency was close, he wrote to his English friend James Maury that although their two countries were about to go to war that did not mean that they were to become personal enemies. Jefferson noted that the 'republic of letters is unaffected by the wars of geographical divisions of the earth,' and therefore drew an important distinction between scientific and political intercourse. Dissolution of the latter did not mean automatic severance of the former.[19] Even when he spoke about the conquest of Canada, Jefferson advanced the need to control the Indians as a rationale, much the same argument he had used in urging American control of the Floridas. Jefferson's militancy, although it had imperial overtones, could not mask his view of war as a limited political instrument.

At times, Jefferson's sense of restraint underwent severe strain and even collapsed. He indulged in some wildly unrealistic thinking about the martial capabilities of his country, even though he freely confessed American military ignorance. 'The acquisition of Canada this year, as far as the neighborhood of Quebec, will be a mere matter of marching, and will give us experience for the attack of Halifax the next, and the final expulsion of England from the American continent.'[20] If the British dared to burn New York or Boston, then the United States could hire incendiaries in England to scorch London. But Jefferson hoped the Americans would confine themselves to the conquest of British North America and to the defence of their own borders. Conquest proved impossible in the early stages of the fighting, and the Americans were barely able to hold their own in the second full year of the war. But Jefferson declared extravagantly that he had known 'no war entered into under more favourable auspices.' He was delighted to learn that the Orders-in-Council had been withdrawn, but the war had to continue. It took more to stop fighting than merely prevent it, he stated, and added theatrically: 'the sword once drawn, full justice must be done.'[21]

Impressment was the central issue and when news of the peace treaty contained nothing on this point he declaimed that 'we must sacrifice the last dollar and drop of blood to rid us of that badge of slavery; and it must rest with England alone to say whether it is worth eternal war, for eternal it must be if she holds to the wrong.'[22] He also fumed against incompetent generals who seemed to surrender their armies to foes a fraction of their strength in Canada and hoped they would be cashiered or shot so that better men could come to the fore. The country had to persevere. It must recover its due rank. Jefferson made several suggestions for the conduct of the war through Madison, but his remarks were politely ignored.[23] The Madison administration made its own mistakes.

Jefferson responded to the reality of war much as he had during the Revolution. He was outraged by British 'savagery,' especially their use of Indian allies. The burning of Washington was a wanton violation of the rules of civilized warfare, and he accepted rumours that it was an 'habitual' British practice to violate women and brutalize prisoners.[24] His arguments for conquest and retaliatory scorching of London notwithstanding, Jefferson was horrified when warfare moved outside the boundaries supposedly established by civilized conduct. The financial costs also seemed excessive: 'Farewell all hope of extinguishing the public debt! Farewell all visions of applying the surplus revenue to the improvements of peace, rather than the ravages of war. Our enemy has indeed the consolation of Satan on removing our first parents from Paradise; from a peaceful and agricultural nation he makes us a military and manufacturing one.'[25] War seemed a lamentable engine of historical change for Jefferson, grinding down his hopes for the American future.

But the War of 1812 ended happily for the Americans. If the peace negotiators at Ghent were uncertain about their work, it was well received and they gave nothing away. In retrospect, the war became a palliative and purge, and, important dissent notwithstanding, it created a new sense of national unity. Jefferson was pleased, but thought that the Treaty of Ghent would be a mere truce, 'to be terminated by the first act of impressment committed on an American citizen.'[26] His Anglophobia remained, despite the downfall and exile of Napoleon which erased the principal causes of Anglo-American discord. But the tyrant of the oceans stood undefeated, although chastised in Jefferson's view, and mightier than ever without the counterbalancing effect of Napoleon.[27]

Jefferson did not realize that the British government was moving into a new era in its foreign relations. A succession of foreign ministers, beginning with Lord Castlereagh, would carve out an Anglo-American understanding with a succession of suspicious but willing Americans. Danger momentarily returned when Napoleon escaped from Elba and embarked on the Hundred Days' adventure, and Jefferson wrote at once that the 'gauntlet must be forever hurled' at any power which questioned America's right to freedom of the seas.[28] These issues were dead, however, because the British had no intention of antagonizing the Americans further, and Napoleon was swiftly dispatched at the suitably climactic Battle of Waterloo. The Anglo-American peace was secure, Jefferson's alarmism notwithstanding.

Jefferson developed a salutary view of the War of 1812 in time. He rejoiced over Andrew Jackson's victory at New Orleans, even though it came after the signing of the treaty, and believed that the United States had made Britain 'better estimate the value of our peace.' The war had also shown that America would fight when necessary to protect her self-respect.[29] He told Lafayette in 1817 that the increased debt from the war was a cheap price to pay for the establishment of 'necessary manufactures,' evidently forgetting his earlier views on cost. But more important, 'proof that our government is solid, can stand the shock of war, and is superior even to civil schism, are precious facts to us ...' [30] Despite its burdens, the war came to have positive value for Jefferson.

Jefferson's nationalism ensured that any sense of ideological solidarity with other nations counted considerably less than the survival and independence of his own. Even though he believed that the United States had both material and spiritual interests in the Latin American rebellions which began in 1808 and went on intermittently for nearly two decades, he denied that his country should become involved in the conflicts and cautioned against a too-hasty recognition of rebel governments to avoid antagonizing Spain. The events in Latin America were a family affair, and when one side had firmly established its rights by force, then it would be time enough for American recognition.[31] Dabbling in the Latin American revolutions might bring a commitment which could lead to war and threaten American interests in the Floridas or the southwest. Jefferson's strongly pragmatic approach to foreign policy meant that he eschewed international crusades.

Jefferson's political xenophobia extended beyond traditional Anglophobia and fear of the major powers. It was inherent in his republicanism. 'What in short is the whole system of Europe towards America but an atrocious and insulting tyranny?' An ocean lay between the two regions, and yet America was made subservient to European laws, regulations, passions, and wars. Whatever happened in South America, truly American governments would develop, 'no longer to be involved in the never-ceasing broils of Europe.' Avoidance of war and proper foreign policy were, as always, interrelated in Jefferson's mind. European wars should never be permitted to send their infectious virus across the oceans to contaminate America.[32] Europe remained an eternal source of war because of her monarchs, excess population, and lack of living space. Her corruption was an eternal threat to American virtue. In America there was hope for peace, but only if the United States could remain a republic independent of entanglements. 'When our strength will permit us to give the law of our hemisphere, it should be that the meridian of the mid-Atlantic should be the line of demarkation between war and peace, on this side of which no act of hostility should be committed, and the lion and the lamb lie down in peace together.'[33] Jefferson even recommended that the United States do without formal commercial treaties, because it could not separate itself too distinctly from the bellicose Europeans, or cultivate its own pacific gardens too assiduously.[34]

Jefferson's belief that Europe was a pit of war seemed well founded in the spring of 1822 when Russia and Turkey, two perennial belligerents, squared off. 'The Cannibals of Europe are going to eating one another again,' he wrote to John Adams, but he consoled himself with the macabre thought that whichever was eliminated would be one less 'destroyer' for the world. When Jefferson learned that French armies had invaded Spain following the constitutionalist revolution there in the same year, and dictated a new form of government, he was outraged. It would be worthwhile for the United States to make its sympathies known but he was not prepared to countenance any close contact with the Old World. Republican idealism necessitated American non-involvement: 'They are nations of eternal war. All their energies are expended in the destruction of the labor, property and lives of their people. On our part, never had a people so favourable a chance of trying the opposite system, of peace and fraternity with mankind, and the direction of all our means and faculties to the purpose of improvement instead of destruction.'[35]

Not surprisingly, a series of letters passed between president James Monroe and the Sage of Monticello about the British proposal which led to the Monroe Doctrine. Jefferson was initially equivocal. America needed a separate system so that her hemisphere could become a haven of freedom, but there was certainly no harm in cultivating England's friendship. Jefferson would not purchase this at the price of entering her wars, but a struggle to prevent the re-establishment of monarchical governments in Latin America would be one which was close to the heart of vital American interests. In short, Jefferson recommended guarded acceptance.[36] The basic components of Monroe's doctrine – mutual non-intervention, no future colonization, and non-transfer of New World colonies – had been features of American foreign policy since the 1790s. Jefferson, Monroe, John Quincy Adams, and many other American statesmen spoke the same language on this subject. They all attempted to avoid European wars by following a foreign policy of political neutrality. They had no intention of risking entanglement in any martial disputes which did not reflect the immediate vital interests of their country.

Many of the broad themes of Jefferson's view of war seemed to come together, like his nationalism, republicanism, and isolationism, during the years of his rustication. He seems to have always viewed war as an instrument of politics, not moral salvation. Notwithstanding his belief that there was a moral law which ought to govern all nations, Jefferson did not envisage stepping beyond the boundaries of the western hemisphere: '... for us to attempt a war to reform all Europe, and bring them back to principles of morality and a respect for the equal rights of nations, would show us to be only maniacs of another character.'[37]

This was why he avoided the Latin American rebellions. True, he argued for the expulsion of Britain from North America and for universal military training in terms reminiscent of the *levée en masse* of the French Revolution.[38] On the surface, these points contradict the argument that Jefferson saw war as a limited instrument of policy. But the temper of the war years made his urge for conquest intelligible, and the models he evoked for making every citizen a soldier were drawn from Greece and Rome, not the decree of the Convention of 23 August 1793, which had called for the *levée en masse*. He accepted a continued British presence in North America, viewing impressment as the central issue, and his attitudes towards defence policy were postulated on abhorrence of debt and republican fears of a standing army.

Jefferson had come around to the conclusion that war was a part of nature, occasionally both just and necessary. War certainly seemed to be the 'natural state of man' in Europe.[39] But the 'pugnacious humor of mankind' also seemed to be one of the laws of man's nature, 'one of the obstacles to too great multiplication provided in the mechanism of the Universe.' War was a losing game to both parties, but all men knew that unless they resisted encroachment at some point 'all will be taken from them' and more would be lost by submission than resistance. This argument encompassed both pragmatic and spiritual values, but Jefferson tended to emphasize the pragmatic. It was a case of giving a limb to save a life. 'It is the melancholy law of human societies to be compelled to choose a great evil in order to ward off a greater; to deter their neighbours from rapine by making it cost them more than honest gains.'[40] As with the embargo, Jefferson still placed great reliance on material self-interest to produce security. He was still too rational in his expectations.

Jefferson always hoped for a peaceful world, but he did not believe that violence could be banished from human affairs, Enlightenment optimist though he was. When the pacifist Noah Worcester sent some peace pamphlets early in 1816, Jefferson thanked him politely and agreed that if nations entered war to avenge slighted honour, much as a man engaged in a duel, this created conflicts that were 'needless, unjust, inhuman, as well as anti-Christian.' But Jefferson did not agree with Worcester that war never resulted in gain. He offered the recent contest with Britain as testimony that an aggressor who suffered a significant loss would think twice about future depredations. Nearly two years later, Jefferson reminded Worcester that he had been personally disposed to maintain peace as long as possible, as the world well knew. Jefferson hoped, 'by improving the mind and morals of society, to lessen the disposition to war,' but he despaired of its abolition. Nevertheless, he cheerfully accepted enrolment in the membership of Worcester's society. He believed it would show his dedication to peace '... and although I dare not promise myself that it can be perpetually maintained, yet if, by the inculcations of reason or religion, the perversities of our nature can be so far corrected as sometimes to prevent the necessity, either supposed or real, of an appeal to the blinder scourges of war, murder, and devastation, the benevolent endeavors of the friends of peace will not be entirely without remuneration.'[41]

Once again, Jefferson revealed his conviction that the impulse to war lay imbedded in human nature and human perceptions. He was of the same optimistic cast of mind as the pacifists but less sanguine in his ultimate hopes. He thought men capable of indefinite, rather than infinite, improvement. In this way Jefferson remained firmly cemented in the pragmatism of the Enlightenment. He never fell into the euphoria of romantic perfectionism which had such a great appeal to the American mind in the early nineteenth century. Jefferson was no pacifist because he was willing to cross into the realm of thought where wars were necessary, just, lawful, and even useful in the scheme of nature.[42] No true pacifist could ever hold such a position.

Jefferson continued to accept the trinity of commerce, war, and debt. His autarkic thinking had emerged in the 1780s when he had asserted that restricted commerce would promote peace. But this was also part of his developing isolationism and an occasional scapegoat for his frustrations over America's entanglement with world politics, despite her own wishes. The enormous debt under which the British taxpayer groaned stemmed from England's many commercial wars and Jefferson shuddered at the thought of the United States ever acquiring such a burden. Although he became reconciled to the presence of manufacturing, he did not believe its production should go beyond immediate needs. Commerce should only dispose of agricultural surpluses, he thought, betraying little understanding of trade relations. Commerce would 'increase our dependence on foreign nations, and our liability to war.' It might produce employment, but also 'wars, debt, and dilapidation,' he wrote to Jean-Baptiste Say, one of the new breed of economic thinkers who argued that freer and more extended trade, not one with autarkic shackles, would lead to peace. Say must have shaken his head in bemusement over the naïveté of the famous American.[43] But from Jefferson's perspective, such a view was wisdom, as was a strict separation of the new and old worlds. Even though he wanted international co-operation to suppress piracy and the slave trade, Jefferson thought that Europe and America should each police only its home waters. 'In this way those collisions would be avoided between the vessels of war of different nations, which beget wars and constitute the weightiest objections to navies.'[44] In his heart, Jefferson never jettisoned the China simile he had once used when asked what policy he would recommend for his country.

The link between war and debt in conjunction with the notion of discrete generations was another idea that Jefferson never abandoned. He advanced several elaborate schemes to cushion the long-range financial impact of the War of 1812. The earth belonged to the living and the generation which contracted a war should be compelled to pay for it.[45] Over the issue of avoiding war with Spain, which might arise from a premature recognition of Latin American republics, Jefferson noted that '... our right may be doubted of mortgaging posterity for the expences of a war in which they will have a right to say their interests are not concerned. It is incumbent on every generation to pay its own debts as it goes. A principle, which, if acted on, would save one half the wars of the world ...'[46]

With occasional lapses, Jefferson was a pacific man through most of his life. He never denied, however, that force was a final arbiter, and this belief persisted during his declining years as he reflected on the needs of his country and the condition of man. He retained the view that war was a rational instrument of policy, to be used for limited objectives only after cautious consideration. Once engaged, he drew a sharp distinction between civilized and savage warfare. Rules and laws should govern all human activity, even war. Against a brutal enemy, he argued that it was better to endure than succumb to retaliation in kind, even though he had done just that with Henry Hamilton during the Revolution and threatened to scorch London if the British burned coastal cities during the War of 1812. Still, there is no reason to doubt the sincerity of his view that it was 'more honorable and more profitable too, to set a good example than to follow a bad one.' The analysis made in the parlour is often somewhat more refined than the decision made in the heat of battle. But this remark reflected the sense of restraint and discipline inherent in the eighteenth-century view of war. Forbearance was the principal alternative to hostilities in Jefferson's view, even though he had never failed to recommend war when pressed to the wall. He had set a model example of restraint in the face of provocation, and thus qualifies as a half-way pacifist. He hoped that example would have moral coercive power just as he hoped that economic interdiction would strike at material self-interest to produce reason in an antagonist. But he accepted war as the ultimate recourse if these alternatives failed.[47]

War is both natural and factitious. Man's personal pugnacity notwithstanding, his wars are to a great extent artificial. They are based on manufactured fears, ambitions, or desires, and by virtue of the organization required for their initiation and execution, they are the result of conscious choice and determination, as Jefferson realized. For example, he did not believe that war was a justified response to the *Chesapeake-Leopard* affair, although it was probably his for the asking. Neither did he believe even limited reprisal was a proper response to French depredations after 1795, although John Adams did. Both men were guided by their belief about what was appropriate policy under the circumstances, and belief, to some extent, determined whether war took place or not. Jefferson grew out of an age which persuaded its statesmen to be circumspect about utilizing violence to redress grievances. Every possible recourse had to be exhausted first. Once declared, war must be conducted in a civilized manner, not after the fashion of barbarians. War was to coerce an antagonist, not exterminate him. As a result, wars prior to the French Revolution and after the Religious Wars of the sixteenth century were conducted in a restrained manner, with minimum loss of life and damage to society and its property. When nationalist passions gripped men's imaginations, and the enemy became a symbol of evil, restraint collapsed. War has been elastic in nature and this has derived in large measure from the perceptions of the men who contemplate its use and conduct its operations.

Two of the most important military analysts for the modern age, Karl von Clausewitz and Baron Henri de Jomini, grew out of the same intellectual background which shaped Jefferson's beliefs. The differences between the American and the Europeans are legion, but they shared common assumptions about war. To Jomini, war was an integral part of civilization. A true Enlightenment figure, he sought order in the chaos of nature through the laws which seemed to govern war's operation. Much of his work was highly technical, but he believed that war was capable of control and manipulation as a rational instrument of policy. Jomini deplored the excesses of the Napoleonic struggles. He found their fanaticism difficult to accept or comprehend, and expressed a longing for the restrained and civilized warfare of the eighteenth century.[48]

Clausewitz was of a like mind, although he transcended the eighteenth-century framework to a more ethereal realm in his analysis of war. But while he asserted that war was an act of violence which, by its very nature, could not be constrained, Clausewitz accepted it only as a means to an end: it was always an instrument of policy, and as such controllable to some degree. All wars were on a continuum in Clausewitz's thinking, with limitation at one end and totality at the other. But he drew a sharp distinction between the two extremes. If a state began a conflict for a limited objective, this did not mean automatic escalation to total war.[49]

Jefferson's view of war was essentially similar. He viewed it as a tool to be manipulated, although he did not engage in the systematic and probing analysis of either Jomini or Clausewitz. His policies, both as advocator and executor, reveal the same concern for national security and prosperity that later guided Bismarck during the wars he engineered for German unification. His basic criterion for judging the efficacy of an American war was to what extent it served the interests of the United States. To be sure, Jefferson lacked the cynical guile of the German chancellor, but his basic perception of war was much the same. Jefferson occasionally collapsed before the irrational tides which sweep about in any war, but these were only fleeting lapses, because he remained fundamentally a man of restraint, civility, and strong moral principles.

It might seem blatantly self-evident to suggest that more attention must be paid to the perceptions of statesmen in order to understand the American military experience, but remarkably few historians have grappled with the American approach to war, except for the period of the Cold War. And many of them have asserted that Americans have not waged wars for policy, but approached their martial conflicts as crusades. Edward McNall Burns stated boldly that in America force had '... always been considered a justifiable instrument for the attainment of those noble purposes which Destiny has thrust upon us. As the Israelites of the modern world we could hardly think otherwise. The Chosen People have a God-given right to put to the sword those who would prevent us from extending the sphere of our blessings.'[50] Burns was arguing a special thesis, but his point was clear and it has been echoed elsewhere. An American army officer, T.B. Kittredge, asserted that it was almost impossible for Americans to fight limited wars because they had not recognized war as a political act, rather as a crusade. Samuel P. Huntington agreed, and placed Jefferson squarely in an American liberal tradition which took a moral view of war: 'Since liberalism deprecates the moral validity of the interests of the state in security, war must be either condemned as incompatible with liberal goals or justified as a movement in support of those goals. American thought has not viewed war in the conservative-military sense as an instrument of national policy.'[51]

John Shy, Russell Weigley, and Bernard Brodie, all perceptive students of the American military experience, agree. Shy, who has mated learning theory with history, argues that since the colonial era the American call for a total solution in war has been continually reinforced by success. Weigley is more concerned with strategic thought, but also maintains that Americans have historically tended to look for total solutions in their military encounters. Brodie dissects American wars in the twentieth century while arguing that the problems have arisen because the leaders of the United States have consistently failed to heed the lessons of Clausewitz. The only dissenting voice is that of Walter Millis. He stated that although Americans initiated the era of people's wars in the Revolution their mentality before the Civil War remained that of the eighteenth century.[52] The consensus is that Americans have been anti- or non-Clausewitzian.

This study of Jefferson's view of war suggests that such an interpretation may be in need of revision. Certainly Jefferson, and by implication many of his contemporaries and colleagues, saw war as an instrument to be used in the national political interest or avoided for the same reason. This related directly to their perception of the correct foreign policy for their young and vulnerable country. Although he had a defensive mentality common to most Americans of this period, Jefferson actively used violence either directly or implicitly in his policies against the Barbary pirates, Spain, England, and France to maintain his country's independence and security. He argued that wars should only be in the interests of the people, and constantly sought the consent of the legislature for his action, but he believed that he understood his country's interests best, as his embargo and reaction to the Quasi-War suggest. He was more a pragmatist than a pacifist and continually weighed possible risks and gains. None of this contradicted his republican optimism or ideology. If Jefferson seems a proto-Clausewitzian, it is because he emerged from the same age, with many of the same assumptions about the use of war, and he consistently operated on the basis of those assumptions while in and out of public office. Jefferson viewed war through the spectacles provided by the thinking of the eighteenth century, which made him at once optimistic about the control of war but distinctly pessimistic about ever seeing its elimination from human affairs.

Notes

CHAPTER 1: REVOLUTIONARY AND DIPLOMAT

1   TJ to George Gilmer, 5 July 1775, Julian P. Boyd, ed., *The Papers of Thomas Jefferson* (Princeton 1950-), I, 186; to James Madison, 8 Feb. 1786, *ibid.*, IX, 264. Hereafter cited as *Papers*

2   TJ 'Draught of Instructions,' *ibid.*, I, 133

3   Willard M. Wallace, *Appeal to Arms: A Military History of the American Revolution* (New York 1951), 17-18; Don Higginbotham, *The War of American Independence: Military Attitudes, Policies, and Practice, 1763-1789* (New York 1971), 45-8, 59-61

4   Frank L. Mott, 'The Newspaper Coverage of Lexington and Concord,' *New England Quarterly*, XVII (1944), 489-505; Arthur M. Schlesinger, *Prelude to Independence: The Newspaper War on Britain, 1764-1776* (New York 1965), 231-49

5   TJ to Francis Eppes, 26 June 1775, *Papers*, I, 174

6   TJ to Gilmer, 5 July 1775, *ibid.*, 186

7   See Julian P. Boyd, 'The Disputed Authorship of the Declaration on the Causes and Necessity for Taking Up Arms, 1775,' *Pennsylvania Magazine of History and Biography*, LXXIV (1950), 51-73. For Jefferson's and Dickinson's draughts, the final copy adopted by Congress, and explanatory notes, see *Papers*, I, 187-217.

8   *Ibid.*, 193-8, for Jefferson's composition draught. Walter Millis, *Arms and Men: A Study of American Military History* (New York 1956), 22-3. Citations for the just war are legion. Good surveys are Joachim von Elbe, 'The Evolution of the Concept of the Just War in International Law,' *American Journal of International Law*, XXX (1939), 665-88, and Brian Bond, 'The "Just War" in Historical Perspective,' *History Today*, XVI (1966), 111-19.

9   Worthington Chauncey Ford, ed., *Journals of the Continental Congress, 1774-1789* (Washington, DC 1905), IV, 229-33. Hereafter cited as *Journals of Congress*

10 TJ to John Randolph, 29 Nov. 1775, *Papers*, I, 269

11 See William B. Ballis, *The Legal Position of War: Changes in Its Practise and Theory from Plato to Vattel* (The Hague 1936)

12 Robert D. Heinl, Jr., *Dictionary of Military and Naval Quotations* (Annapolis 1966), 340, 346

13 TJ to John Page, 5 Aug. 1776, *Papers*, I, 485-6. See Jack M. Sosin, 'The Use of Indians in the War of the American Revolution: A Re-Assessment of Responsibility,' *Canadian Historical Review*, XLVI (1965), 101-21

14 John U. Nef, *War and Human Progress: An Essay on the Rise of Industrial Civilization* (New York 1963), 185, 191-2, 200-1; Roland Bainton, *Christian Attitudes toward War and Peace* (New York 1960), 174-82; Peter Gay, *The Enlightenment: An Interpretation* (New York 1969), II, 37-41

15 TJ to Patrick Henry, 27 March 1779, *Papers*, II, 242. *Ibid.*, 255; Felix Gilbert, *To the Farewell Address: Ideas of Early American Foreign Policy* (Princeton 1961), 44-75; Daniel J. Boorstin, *The Lost World of Thomas Jefferson* (New York 1948), 146; Adrienne Koch, *The Philosophy of Thomas Jefferson* (New York 1943), 19-20, 30; Dumas Malone, *Jefferson the Virginian* (Boston 1948), 178

16 TJ to Theodorick Bland, 8 June 1779, *Papers*, II, 286-7. See Leonard J. Kramer, 'Muskets in the Pulpit, 1776-1783,' *Presbyterian Historical Society Journal*, XXXII (1954), 38, for a clerical perspective.

17 TJ to George Washington, 17 July 1779, *Papers*, III, 40; to William Phillips, 22 July 1779, *ibid.*, 44, 45-6. Retaliation was accepted as part of natural law. Emerich de Vattel, *The Law of Nations*, trans. Charles G. Fenwick (Washington, DC 1916), 280-1. For Vattel's influence, see Jesse Reeves, 'The Influence of the Law of Nature upon International Law in the United States,' *American Journal of International Law*, III (1909), 549.

18 'Advice of Council respecting Henry Hamilton and Others,' in Council, 29 Sept. 1779, *Papers*, III, 94-5

19 TJ to Washington, 2 Oct. 1779, *ibid.*, 99; to George Matthews, 8 Oct. 1779, *ibid.*, 101-3

20 TJ to George Rogers Clark, 1 Jan. 1780, *ibid.*, 259

21 TJ to James Wood, 17 Nov. 1780, *ibid.*, IV, 101. To Washington, 26 Nov. 1780, *ibid.*, 163-4

22 *Ibid.*, 257. Elizabeth Cometti, 'The Governorship of Thomas Jefferson,' PH D dissertation, Department of History, University of Virginia, 1934. Cometti, 'Depredations in Virginia during the Revolution,' in Darrett B. Rutman, ed., *The Old Dominion: Essays for Thomas Perkins Abernethy* (Charlottesville 1964), 131-51, discusses the impact of war on Virginia.

23 *Papers*, IV, 487-8

24 *Ibid.*, 653

25 TJ to Phillips, March 1781, *ibid.*, V, 227. See also to George Weedon, 10 April 1781, *ibid.*, 401-2. Jefferson was not above subterfuge himself. See Lyman H. Butterfield, 'Psychological Warfare in 1776: The Jefferson-Franklin Plan to Cause Hessian Desertions,' *American Philosophical Society Proceedings*, XCIV (1950), 233-41

26 *Papers*, VI, 61. Injury meant any denial of what was rightfully the individual's by the law of nature – life, liberty, or property. Vattel, *Law of Nations*, 228-9, 243; John Locke, *Two Treatises of Government*, ed. Peter Laslett (Cambridge 1960), 296-7, 388-9; Hugo Grotius, *The Rights of War and Peace*, trans. A.C. Campbell (New York 1911), 75, 76, 83, 245

27 *Papers*, VI, 393-400. See also Vattel, *Law of Nations*, 284; *Journals of Congress*, XXV, 821-35

28 TJ, 'Notes on the State of Virginia,' Paul Leicester Ford, ed., *The Works of Thomas Jefferson* (New York 1905), III, 438-9; IV, 28, 98-9. Hereafter cited as *Works*

29 *Ibid.*, IV 100. See also Reginald C. Stuart, 'Thomas Jefferson and the Origins of War,' *Peace and Change*, IV (1977), 22-7

30 See references in *Papers*, VI, 471-2, 540. TJ to Benjamin Harrison, 3 March, and to James Madison, 11 Nov. 1784, *ibid.*, VII, 502; to David Humphreys, 18 Sept. 1787, *ibid.*, XII, 33

31 Richard Joseph McCarthy, 'Some Philosophical Foundations of Thomas Jefferson's Foreign Policy,' PH D dissertation, Department of History, St John's University, New York, 1958, 191-2, 197

32 TJ to C.W.F. Dumas, 6 May 1786, *Papers*, IX, 462-3. For China reference, see to G.K. van Hogendorp, 13 Oct. 1785, *ibid.*, VIII, 633.

33 TJ to John Jay, 23 Aug. 1785, *ibid.*, 427; to Washington, 4 Nov. 1788, *ibid.*, XIV, 328

34 TJ to Wilson Miles Cary, 12 Aug. 1787, *ibid.*, XII, 24. See also to David Rittenhouse, 18 Sept. 1787, *ibid.*, 145

35 TJ to Nicholas Lewis, 29 July 1787, *ibid.*, XI, 640

36 TJ to William Carmichael, 25 Sept. 1787, *ibid.*, XII, 174

37 Adrienne Koch, *Jefferson and Madison: The Great Collaboration* (New York 1964), 62-96; Julian P. Boyd, 'Editorial Note,' *Papers*, XV, 384-93; McCarthy, 'Foundations of Jefferson's Foreign Policy,' 27-8

38 TJ to John Rutledge, 6 Aug. 1787, *Papers*, XI, 701. Jefferson became quite disturbed over this threatened war. See to James Monroe, 5 Aug. 1787, and to David Humphreys, 14 Aug. 1787, *ibid.*, XI, 687, and XII, 33

39 TJ to Madison, 6 Sept. 1789, *ibid.*, XV, 397

40 McCarthy, 'Foundations of Jefferson's Foreign Policy,' 120. Montesquieu, *The Spirit of Laws*, trans. Thomas Nugent (Chicago 1952), 59, 60, 64-5, emphasizes the tendency of monarchs to wage war. This was a common theme of the Enlightenment. Elizabeth V. Souleyman, *The Vision of World Peace in Seventeenth and*

Eighteenth-Century France (New York 1941), 34, 45, 57

41 TJ to Monroe, 11 Nov. 1784, *Papers*, VII, 511-12; to Horatio Gates, 13 Dec. 1784, *ibid.*, 571

42 TJ to Monroe, 6 Feb. 1785, *ibid.*, 639-40

43 TJ to Jay, 23 Aug. 1785, *ibid.*, VIII, 427. See also J.G. de Roulhac Hamilton, 'The Pacifism of Thomas Jefferson,' *Virginia Quarterly Review*, XXXI (1955), 611-14; McCarthy, 'Foundations of Jefferson's Foreign Policy,' 224 ff. Jefferson noted that revenge was a natural privilege in both criminal law and society: in Gilbert Chinard, ed., *The Commonplace Book of Thomas Jefferson: A Repertory of His Ideas on Government* (Baltimore 1926), 97-9.

44 TJ to Madison, 8 Feb. 1786, *Papers*, IX, 264

45 TJ to Jay, 3 Nov. 1787, *ibid.*, XII, 312. This theme emerged as an issue in the pressures leading to the adoption of the Constitution of 1787. See Frederick W. Marks, III, 'Foreign Affairs: A Winning Issue in the Campaign for the Ratification of the United States Constitution,' *Political Science Quarterly*, LXXXVI (1971), 444-69

46 TJ to Washington, 4 Nov. 1788, *Papers*, XIV, 328

47 TJ to Adams, 11 July 1786, *ibid.*, VIII, 123-4, 176-8, and IX, 64, 611-12, for other TJ-Adams correspondence on this point. Jefferson never discarded this view. TJ, 'Autobiography,' in *Works*, I, 99

48 The American Commissioners to Vergennes, 28 March 1785, *Papers*, VIII, 62

49 TJ to Adams, 27 Nov. 1785, *ibid.*, IX, 64, and to Monroe, 11 Aug. 1786, *ibid.*, X, 224

50 TJ, 'Proposed Convention against the Barbary States,' 4 July 1786, and 'Proposed Confederation against the Barbary States,' ca. Oct. 1786, *ibid.*, X, 566-8, 569-70

51 Boyd, 'Editorial Note,' *ibid.*, 562-4

52 Motion by William Grayson, seconded by John Kean, 27 July 1786, *Journals of Congress*, XXXIII, 419-20

53 Jay to Congress, 2 Aug. 1787, *ibid.*, 452-3. Boyd, 'Editorial Note' to TJ, 'Reports on Mediterranean Trade and Algerine Captives,' *Papers*, XVIII, 390-6

54 Boyd, 'Editorial Note,' in *ibid.*, X, 585-6. TJ to Jay, 11 Aug. 1788, *ibid.*, XIII, 500-1; John Paul Jones to TJ, 26 Jan. 1789, *ibid.*, XIV, 506. For Franklin's views, see Benjamin Franklin, 'On War and Peace,' *Old South Leaflets* (New York n.d.), VII, 225-43. For eighteenth-century peace literature, see M.C. Jacob, ed., *Peace Projects of the Eighteenth Century* (New York 1974), Carl J. Friedrich, *Inevitable Peace* (Cambridge, Mass. 1948), and Souleyman, *Vision of Peace*. Sylvester John Hemleben, *Plans for World Peace through Six Centuries* (New York 1972), places eighteenth-century thinking in perspective.

55 'Instructions to the Commissioners Negotiating Treaties of Amity and Commerce,' 2 April 1784, *Journals of Congress*, XXVI, 181-2. See *Papers*, VII, 261-71, for Jefferson's copy.

56 Vattel, *Law of Nations*, 259-60, 278-335 *passim*. For a reference to Vattel and Wolff

by TJ see to Monroe, 10 May 1784, *Papers*, VII, 240, fn 1. See also Reeves, 'Influence of the Law of Nature,' and Charles G. Fenwick, 'The Authority of Vattel,' *American Political Science Review*, VII (1913), 395-410

57 Boyd, 'Editorial Note' to 'Jefferson's "General Form" of a Treaty,' 4 Sept. to 10 Nov. 1784, *Papers*, VII, 463-70. TJ, 'Classification of Treaty Provisions,' *ibid.*, 476-8; 'Draft of a Model Treaty,' *ibid.*, 482-3. The clause on a period of grace for merchants was written into the Treaty of Amity and Commerce with France (1778) and the Treaty of Peace and Commerce with the Netherlands (1780). See Senate Documents, *Treaties, Conventions, International Acts, Protocols and Agreements between the United States of America and Other Powers, 1776-1909*, comp. William M. Malloy (Washington, DC 1910), I, 475, and II, 1239. Hereafter cited as *Treaties*

58 The American commissioners to De Thulemeier, 10 Nov. 1784, *Papers*, VII, 490-1

59 'Enclosure,' *ibid.*, 491-2. *Treaties*, II, 1484-5, for Prussian treaty. See *ibid.*, I, 1209, 1211, for relevant provisions in the 1787 treaty with Morocco, and *ibid.*, 1732-3, 1747, for the same in a 1783 treaty with Sweden.

60 Jay to Gouverneur Morris, 24 Sept. 1783, Henry P. Johnston, ed., *The Correspondence and Public Papers of John Jay* (New York 1891), III, 84

CHAPTER 2: DIPLOMAT AND POLITICIAN

1 Barnard, *A Sermon Preached at the Request of the Antient and Honourable Artillery Company in Boston* (Boston 1789), 27-8. Evans #21669, in Clifford L. Shipton, ed., *Early American Imprints* (Worcester Mass.). TJ to Elbridge Gerry, 21 June 1797, Paul Leicester Ford, ed., *The Works of Thomas Jefferson* (New York 1905), VIII, 313

2 Lawrence S. Kaplan, *Jefferson and France: An Essay on Politics and Political Ideas* (New Haven 1967), 38-40, 51-3

3 John Rutledge, Jr., to TJ, 6 May 1790, Julian P. Boyd, ed., *The Papers of Thomas Jefferson* (Princeton 1950-), XVI, 413-15; William Short to John Jay, 11 May 1790, *ibid.*, 425-6; Rutledge to TJ, 12 May 1790, *ibid.*, 426-8

4 TJ to Edward Rutledge, 4 July 1790, *ibid.*, 601; to Benjamin Vaughan, 27 June 1790, *ibid.*, 580; to Francis Eppes, 4 July 1790, *ibid.*, 598; and to George Gilmer, 25 July 1790, *ibid.*, XVII, 269. The fortunes of American trade are traced in Anna Cornelia Caulder, *American Commerce as Affected by the Wars of the French Revolution and Napoleon, 1793-1812* (Philadelphia 1932).

5 Samuel Flagg Bemis, 'Thomas Jefferson: Secretary of State,' in Bemis, ed., *The American Secretaries of State and Their Diplomacy* (New York 1927), II, 41-3; Julian P. Boyd, *Number 7: Alexander Hamilton's Secret Attempts to Control American Foreign Policy* (Princeton 1964), 65

6 TJ to James Monroe, 11 July 1790, *Papers*, XVII, 25, and to Thomas Mann Randolph, Jr., 11 July 1790, *ibid.*, 26

7 TJ, 'Outline of Policy on the Mississippi Question,' 2 Aug. 1790, *ibid.*, 113-16

8 TJ to Short, 10 Aug. 1790, *ibid.*, 121-3; Bemis, 'Jefferson,' 41-3; Boyd, *Number 7*, 65

9 TJ, 'Outline of Policy,' 2 Aug. 1790, *Papers*, XVII, 116; Secretary of State to Gouverneur Morris, 12 Aug. 1790, *ibid.*, 127-8

10 Morris cited in Lawrence S. Kaplan, *Colonies into Nation: American Diplomacy, 1763-1801* (New York 1972), 197

11 TJ, 'First Opinion of the Secretary of State,' 28 Aug. 1790, *Papers*, XVII, 129-32, 136-61

12 TJ to Morris, 26 Nov. 1790, *ibid.*, XVIII, 82. See also to Francis Kinloch, 26 Nov. 1790, *ibid.*, 80-1

13 TJ to Edward Rutledge, 4 July 1790, *ibid.*, XVI, 600. See also TJ, 'Report on Matters of Negotiation with Spain,' 2 March 1792, *Works*, VI, 397; 'Report on American Trade in the Mediterranean,' 28 Dec. 1790, *Papers*, XVIII, 427-9; 'Report on American Captives in Algiers,' 28 Dec. 1790, *ibid.*, 435

14 TJ, 'Report on Matters of Negotiation with Spain,' 7 and 18 March 1792, *ibid.*, 397, 417-39. See also TJ to William Carmichael, 12 March 1791, *ibid.*, 214-15; to George Nicholas, 22 March 1791, *ibid.*, 223-4; to Short, 18 March 1792, in Andrew A. Lipscomb and Albert Bergh, eds., *The Writings of Thomas Jefferson* (Washington, DC 1903), VIII, 316. Hereafter cited as *Writings*

15 TJ to Monroe, 17 April 1791, *Works*, VI, 242; to the President of the United States, 17 April 1791, *ibid.*, 245

16 TJ to Monroe, 17 April 1791, *ibid.*, 243; to Charles Carroll, 15 April 1791, *Writings*, VIII, 177-8

17 TJ to David Campbell, 27 March 1792, *Works*, VI, 455

18 Merrill D. Peterson, 'Thomas Jefferson and Commercial Policy, 1783-1793,' *William and Mary Quarterly*, 3d Series, XXII (1965), 584-610; Julian P. Boyd, 'Editorial Note,' in *Papers*, XVIII, 220-83 *passim*

19 TJ to Lafayette, 16 June 1792, *Works*, VII, 109. See also Kaplan, *Jefferson and France*, 51; Paul Cox McGrath, 'Secretary Jefferson and Revolutionary France, 1790-1793,' PH D dissertation, Department of History, Boston University, 1950

20 TJ to James Madison, 28 April 1793, *Works*, VII, 302. See also to Joel Barlow, 20 June 1792, *ibid.*, 123, and to Gilmer, 15 Dec. 1792, *ibid.*, 195

21 TJ to Morris, 20 April 1793, *ibid.*, 281-2; TJ, 'The Anas,' *ibid.*, I, 326

22 TJ, 'Opinion on French Treaties,' 28 April 1793, *ibid.*, VII, 283-301 *passim*

23 TJ to Harry Innes, 23 May 1793, *ibid.*, 343. The British also saw the war as a crusade, a point which escaped Jefferson. Alison W. Phillips and Arthur H. Reede, *Neutrality: Its History, Economics and Law* (New York 1936), II, 'The Napoleonic Period,' 7-9

24 TJ to Morris, 16 Aug. 1793, *Works*, VII, 488. See also to Monroe, 14 July 1793, *ibid.*, 447

25 TJ to Madison, 24 March 1793, *ibid.*, 250-1

26 TJ to Thomas Pinckney, 7 May 1793, printed in Carlton Savage, *Policy of the United States toward Maritime Commerce in War* (Washington, DC 1934), I, 163. See also to Pinckney, 7 Sept. 1793, *Works*, VIII, 25; to Messrs Carmichael and Short, in *American State Papers*, eds. Walter Lowrie and Matthew Clarke (Washington, DC 1831-62), Class 1, *Foreign Relations*, I, 265

27 TJ to US commissioners in Spain, 30 June 1793, *Works*, VII, 435; to same, 31 May 1793, *ibid.*, 350-1; to Madison, 23 June 1793, *ibid.*, 408; to Monroe, 28 June 1793, *ibid.*, 415; and to US commissioners in Spain, 30 June 1793, *ibid.*, 424-35 *passim*

28 TJ 'Report on Privileges and Restrictions on the Commerce of the United States in Foreign Countries,' 16 Dec. 1793, *ibid.*, VIII, 114-16

29 TJ to Monroe, 24 April 1794, *ibid.*, 143. See also to Enoch Edwards, 30 Dec. 1793, *ibid.*, 134

30 TJ to Tench Coxe, 1 May 1794, *ibid.*, 147-8

31 TJ to Henry Tazewell, 13 Sept. 1795, *ibid.*, 191. See also to Monroe, 2 March 1793, *ibid.*, 221

32 *Colonies into Nation*, 240

33 TJ to Adams, 28 Dec. 1796, in Lester J. Cappon, ed., *The Adams-Jefferson Letters: The Complete Correspondence between Thomas Jefferson and Abigail and John Adams* (Chapel Hill 1959), I, 263. On Madison's advice this letter was not sent. George Washington, 'Farewell Address,' 17 Sept. 1796, in James D. Richardson, ed., *A Compilation of the Messages and Papers of the Presidents* (New York 1897), I, 214; and 'Annual Address to Congress,' 7 Dec. 1796, *ibid.*, 193

34 See TJ to Archibald Stuart, 14 Jan. 1797, *Works*, VIII, 266-7; to Madison, 22 Jan. 1797, *ibid.*, 272-3

35 TJ to Gerry, 13 May 1797, *ibid.*, 285-6. Jefferson stated that he was willing to go to war rather than separate from his New England 'brethren,' *ibid.*, 287. See also to Doctor John Edwards, 22 Jan. 1797, *ibid.*, 277

36 TJ to Madison, 18 May 1797, *ibid.*, 288-91. See also to Martha Jefferson Randolph, 18 May 1797, in Edwin M. Betts and James A. Bear, Jr., eds., *The Family Letters of Thomas Jefferson* (Columbia, Missouri 1966), 144

37 TJ to Aaron Burr, 17 June 1797, *Works*, VIII, 310-13; to French Strother, 8 June 1797, *ibid.*, 302-3; to Madison, 15 June 1797, *ibid.*, 307-8; to Pinckney, 29 May 1797, *ibid.*, 292

38 TJ to Gerry, 21 June 1797, *ibid.*, 313-14

39 TJ to Pinckney, 29 May 1797, *ibid.*, 293

40 *Ibid.* TJ to Edward Rutledge, 24 June 1797, *ibid.*, 318. Jefferson confessed to Archibald Stuart, 8 June 1798, that he saw no grounds on which to force France to negotiate. *Ibid.*, 438

41 TJ to Peregrine Fitzhugh, 3 Feb. 1798, *ibid.*, 376-7

42 TJ to Horatio Gates, 30 May 1797, *ibid.*, 295; to Edward Rutledge, 24 June 1797, *ibid.*, 318-19

43 TJ to Madison, 29 March and 12 April 1798, *ibid.*, 392-3, 404; to Peter Carr, 12 April 1798, *ibid.*, 406-7; to Colonel Bell, 18 May 1797, *Writings*, IX, 386

44 TJ to Madison, 29 March 1798, *Works*, VIII, 392; to Edmund Pendleton, 2 April 1798, *ibid.*, 396-7

45 TJ to James Lewis, Jr., 9 May 1798, *ibid.*, 417; to Madison, 26 April 1798, *ibid.*, 413

46 TJ to Monroe, 19 April 1798, *ibid.*, 408; to Madison, 19 April 1798, *ibid.*, 410. For citation see to Lewis, 9 May 1798, *ibid.*, 417.

47 TJ to Monroe, 21 March 1798, *ibid.*, 389

48 TJ to Madison, 21 March 1798, *ibid.*, 387; Madison to TJ, 2 April 1798, in Gaillard Hunt, ed., *The Writings of James Madison* (New York 1906), VI, 312-13. Several writers have dealt with this theme recently. See Merlo J. Pusey, *The Way We Go to War* (Boston 1971); Jacob Javits, *Who Makes War: The President versus Congress* (New York 1973); Arthur Schlesinger, Jr., *The Imperial Presidency* (Boston 1973); Charles Lofgren, 'War Making under the Constitution: The Original Understanding,' *Yale Law Journal*, LXXXI (1972), 672-702

49 TJ to Monroe, 23 Jan. 1799, *Works*, IX, 11; to John Page, 24 Jan. 1799, *ibid.*, 13-15

50 TJ to Gerry, 26 Jan. 1799, *ibid.*, 18-24 *passim*

51 TJ to Thomas Lomax, 12 March 1799, *ibid.*, 63. See also to Pendleton, 29 Jan. and 19 Feb. 1799, *ibid.*, 27, 54; to Colonel Nicholas Lewis, 30 Jan. 1799, *Writings*, X, 89

52 TJ to Charles Pinckney, 29 Oct. 1799, *Works*, IX, 87

53 TJ to Gerry, 26 Jan. 1799, *ibid.*, 18-19

54 Merrill D. Peterson, *Thomas Jefferson and the New Nation* (New York 1972), 566-7; William Glenn Moore, 'Economic Coercion as a Policy of the United States, 1794-1805,' PH D dissertation, Department of History, University of Alabama, 1960, 265-7, 279-81

55 TJ to Madison, 1 Jan. 1797, Ford, *Works*, VIII, 264

CHAPTER 3: PRESIDENT AND 'PACIFIST'

1 TJ to Messrs Eddy *et al.*, 27 March 1801, Andrew A. Lipscomb and Albert Bergh, eds., *The Writings of Thomas Jefferson* (Washington, DC 1903), X, 249; to Judge Cooper, 18 Feb. 1806, as cited in Henry Adams, *History of the United States of America during the Administration of Thomas Jefferson* (New York 1930), II, iii, 11

2 John U. Nef, *War and Human Progress* (New York 1963), 315-28; J.F.C. Fuller, *The Conduct of War, 1789-1961* (New Brunswick 1961), 30-1, 44

3 TJ, 'First Annual Message,' 8 Dec. 1801, in James D. Richardson, ed., *A Compilation of the Messages and Papers of the Presidents* (New York 1897), I, 316-17; 'Second Inaugural Address,' 4 March 1805, *ibid.*, 367. Gallatin to TJ, 16 Nov. 1801, Paul Leicester Ford, ed., *The Works of Thomas Jefferson* (New York 1905), IX, 324.

Gallatin to TJ, Nov. 1801, Henry Adams, ed., *The Writings of Albert Gallatin* (Philadelphia 1879), I, 63

4 Dumas Malone, *Jefferson the President: Second Term, 1805-1809* (Boston 1974), 76, for Jefferson's reference to the Constitution, and *ibid.*, 12, 95, 101, for debt and war. TJ to William Short, 3 Oct. 1801, *Works*, IX, 309. TJ to Philip Mazzei, 18 July 1804, *Writings*, XI, 39-40

5 TJ, 'Fifth Annual Message,' 3 Dec. 1805, *Messages and Papers*, I, 373

6 TJ to Benjamin Latrobe, cited in Paul F. Norton, 'Jefferson's Plan for Mothballing the Frigates,' US Naval Institute, *Proceedings*, 82 (1956), 739. See also Julia H. MacLeod, 'Jefferson and the Navy: A Defense,' *Huntington Library Quarterly*, VIII (1945), 170-1, 174-6. Russell F. Weigley, *The American Way of War: A History of United States Military Policy and Strategy* (New York 1973), 45-8, comments on Jefferson's defensive mentality. Mary P. Adams, 'Jefferson's Military Policy with Special Reference to the Frontier, 1805-1809,' PH D dissertation, Department of History, University of Virginia, 1958, is the most extensive study of the subject. Jefferson defended his gunboats at some length to Congress. 10 Feb. 1807, *Messages and Papers*, I, 407-9

7 TJ to the Earl of Buchan, 10 July 1803, *Writings*, X, 401

8 TJ to Madame de Stael-Holstein, 16 July 1807, *ibid.*, XI, 282. To Sir John Sinclair, 30 June 1803, *ibid.*, X, 397; to James Bowdoin, 10 July 1806, *ibid.*, XI, 121

9 TJ to George Logan, 21 March 1801, *Works*, IX, 220; 'First Inaugural Address,' 4 March 1801, *Messages and Papers*, I, 311; to William Duane, 22 March 1806, *Works*, X, 241

10 TJ to Paine, 8 March 1801, *ibid.*, IX, 212-13

11 TJ to Benjamin Rush, 4 Oct. 1803, *ibid.*, X, 32; R.J. McCarthy, 'Some Philosophical Foundations of Thomas Jefferson's Foreign Policy,' PH D dissertation, St. John's University, 1958, 191-2; L.S. Kaplan, *Jefferson and France* (New Haven 1967), 82

12 TJ to Logan, 21 March 1801, *Works*, IX, 220; to Robert Livingston, 9 Sept. 1801, *ibid.*, 300-1; to Emperor Alexander of Russia, 19 April 1806, *ibid.*, X, 250-1; to Monsieur Cabanis, 12 July 1803, *Writings*, X, 405; Henry Adams, *History of the United States of America during the Administration of Thomas Jefferson* (New York 1930), I, i, 212

13 Carlton Savage, *Policy of the United States toward Maritime Commerce in War* (Washington, DC 1934), I, 24-30, 241-4

14 Charles M. Wiltse, *The Jeffersonian Tradition in American Democracy* (Chapel Hill 1935), 196-200; Louis M. Sears, *Jefferson and the Embargo* (New York 1966), chaps. i, ii

15 TJ to James Madison, 15 July 1801, *Works*, IX, 277-8; McCarthy, 'Foundations of Jefferson's Foreign Policy,' 54, 116, 120

16 TJ to Martha Jefferson Randolph, 27 Nov. 1801, E.M. Betts and J.A. Bear, Jr.,

eds., *The Family Letters of Thomas Jefferson* (Columbia, Missouri 1966), 214.
Lawrence S. Kaplan, 'Jefferson, The Napoleonic Wars, and the Balance of Power,' *William and Mary Quarterly*, 3d Series, XIV (1957), 196-217

17 'Instructions to U.S. Ships of War,' 18 Feb. 1802, Dudley W. Knox, ed., *Naval Documents Related to the United States Wars with the Barbary Powers* (Washington, DC 1939-44), II, 60. Gallatin to TJ, 16 Aug. 1802, Henry Adams, ed., *The Writings of Albert Gallatin* (Philadelphia 1879), I, 89; TJ, 'The Anas,' 15 May 1801, 18 Jan. 1802, *Works*, I, 365-6, 370; TJ, 'First Annual Message,' 8 Dec. 1801, *Messages and Papers*, I, 315

18 TJ, 'Fourth Annual Message,' 8 Nov. 1804, *ibid.*, 359

19 TJ to Madison, 22 March 1803, *Works*, IX, 454-5; to Wilson Cary Nicholas, 11 June 1801, *ibid.*, 265; to Judge John Tyler, 29 March 1805, *Writings*, XI, 70

20 Arthur P. Whitaker, *The Mississippi Question, 1795-1803: A Study in Trade, Politics, and Diplomacy* (New York 1934), 198-204; Stuart Seely Sprague, 'Jefferson, Kentucky and the Closing of the Port of New Orleans, 1802-1803,' Kentucky Historical Society, *Register*, LXX (1972), 312-17

21 Mary P. Adams, 'Jefferson's Reaction to the Treaty of San Ildefonso,' *Journal of Southern History*, XXI (1955), 173-88; Dumas Malone, *Jefferson the President: First Term, 1801-1805* (Boston 1970), 255-72

22 *Ibid.*, 281-93. TJ, 'The Anas,' 8 April and 7 May 1803, *Works*, I, 372-3

23 TJ to Livingston, 18 April 1802, *ibid.*, IX, 364-6; to de Nemours, 25 April 1802, Dumas Malone, ed., *Correspondence between Thomas Jefferson and Pierre Samuel DuPont de Nemours, 1798-1817*, trans. Linwood Lehman (Boston 1930), 47. De Nemours understood fully what was expected of him. See de Nemours to TJ, 26 and 30 April 1802, *ibid.*, 49-50, 52-61; TJ to de Nemours, 1 Feb. 1803, *ibid.*, 74-6

24 Adams, *History*, I, i, 445. Malone, *Jefferson, 1801-1805*, 286-7, disagrees.

25 TJ to James Monroe, 13 Jan. 1803, *Works*, IX, 419; to Livingston, 10 Oct. 1802 and 3 Feb. 1803, *ibid.*, 397, 442

26 TJ to Claiborne, 24 May 1803, *Writings*, X, 391-4. See also to Doctor Hugh Williamson, 30 April 1803, *ibid.*, 385-6; to William Dunbar, 3 March 1803, *ibid.*, XIX, 131-2

27 TJ to John Bacon, 30 April 1803, *Works*, IX, 464. See also to Dunbar, 17 July 1803, *ibid.*, X, 19-20; to John Dickinson, 9 Aug. 1803, *ibid.*, 28; to Mazzei, 18 July 1804, *Writings*, XI, 40

28 TJ to Lafayette, 4 Nov. 1803, Gilbert Chinard, ed., *The Letters of Lafayette and Jefferson* (Baltimore 1929), 225. See also TJ to Madison, 14 Sept. 1803, *Works*, X, 30-1; to Gallatin, 29 Oct. 1803, *ibid.*, 45; Gallatin to TJ, 5 Sept. and 28 Oct. 1803, Adams, *Writings of Gallatin*, I, 152-3, 162-6

29 TJ, 'Fifth Annual Message,' 3 Dec. 1805, *Messages and Papers*, I, 372; TJ to Congress, 6 Dec. 1805, *ibid.*, 377; to John Langdon, 22 Dec. 1806, *Writings*, XIX, 157

30 TJ to Monroe, 8 Jan. 1804, *Works*, X, 63; to Madison, 4 Aug. and 27 Aug. 1805, *ibid.*, 168, 172; to de Nemours, 12 Feb. 1806, Malone, *Correspondence*, 89

31 TJ, 'The Anas,' 12 Nov. 1805, *Works*, I, 395-7; to W.C.C. Claiborne, 27 April 1806, *ibid.*, X, 253-6; Everett S. Brown, 'Jefferson's Plan for a Military Colony in Orleans Territory,' *Mississippi Valley Historical Review*, VIII (1922), 373-6

32 TJ to Madison, 16 Aug. 1807, *Works*, X, 476-7. See also to Bowdoin, 2 April 1807, *ibid.*, 381-2. Jefferson argued that Burr had usurped federal prerogatives. 'Proclamation against Burr's Plot,' 27 Nov. 1806, *ibid.*, 301

33 TJ to Madison, 1 Sept. 1807, *ibid.*, 489-90; to Henry Dearborn and Madison, 12 Aug. 1808, *ibid.*, XI, 43, 44; to Gallatin, 9 Aug. 1808, *Writings*, XII, 120-1; Clifford L. Egan, 'The United States, France, and West Florida, 1803-1807,' *Florida Historical Quarterly*, XLVII (1969), 237-50

34 Adams, *History*, II, iv, 138

35 The best study is Bradford Perkins, *Prologue to War: England and the United States, 1805-1812* (Berkeley 1961). In chap. i, he presents an excellent discussion of the British perspective. See also Kaplan, *Jefferson and France*, 129, 197; A.W. Phillips and A.H. Reede, *Neutrality* (New York 1936), II, 113, 179-80

36 TJ, 'Notes on Armed Vessels,' 4 July 1805, *Works*, X, 152-4; 'Proclamation,' 3 May 1806, *Messages and Papers*, I, 390-2. See also to Gallatin, 1 Sept. 1804, *Works*, X, 100, and to John Randolph, 19 Nov. 1804, *ibid.*, 121

37 Herbert Heaton, 'Non-Importation, 1806-1812,' *Journal of Economic History*, I (1941), 178-98; Perkins, *Prologue to War* 109-14; Malone, *Jefferson, 1805-1809*, 396-410

38 TJ to Monroe, 21 March 1807, *Works*, X, 374-7; to Bowdoin, 2 April 1807, *ibid.*, 380-1. Douglas W. Tanner, 'Thomas Jefferson, Impressment, and the Rejection of the Monroe-Pinkney Treaty,' *Essays in History*, XIII (1968), 7-26. TJ, 'The Anas,' 2 Feb. 1807, *Works*, I, 407

39 The best study is Edwin M. Gaines, 'Outrageous Encounter! The Chesapeake Leopard Affair of 1807,' PH D dissertation, Department of History, University of Virginia, 1960

40 TJ, 'Proclamation,' 2 July 1807, *Messages and Papers*, I, 410-12; 'The Anas,' 2 July 1807, *Works*, I, 410; to William Cabell, 24 July and 7 Aug. 1807, *ibid.*, X, 436, 439-40. See also to Madison, 25 Aug. 1807, *ibid.*, 484; to Robert Smith, 18 Sept. 1807, *ibid.*, 497; to Cabell, 19 July 1807, *Writings*, XI, 289; to Madison, 30 Aug. 1807, *ibid.*, 340; to John Nicholas, 17 Aug. 1807, *ibid.*, 332

41 TJ to George Clinton, 6 July 1809, *Works*, X, 449; to Thomas Cooper, 9 July 1807, *ibid.*, 451; to Bowdoin, 10 July 1807, *ibid.*, 454; to Barnabas Bidwell, 10 July 1807, *ibid.*, 456

42 TJ to Cabell, 29 June 1807, *ibid.*, 433

43 TJ to de Nemours, 14 July 1807, Malone, *Correspondence*, 93-4; to Martha Jefferson

Randolph, 27 July 1807, Betts and Bear, *Family Letters*, 311; to Cabell, 16 July 1807, *Writings*, XI, 281; to John Taylor, 1 Aug. 1807, *ibid.*, 304-5

44 Perkins, *Prologue to War*, 146-9. See TJ to William Duane, 20 July 1807, *Works*, X, 471

45 TJ to John W. Eppes, 12 July 1807, *ibid.*, 458. See also 'The Anas,' 1 Dec. 1808, *ibid.*, I, 429; to Short, 15 Nov. 1807, *Writings*, XI, 393. Mary Adams, 'Jefferson's Military Policy,' 183-92

46 For background, see W.G. Moore, 'Economic Coercion as a Policy of the United States, 1794-1805,' PH D dissertation, University of Alabama, 1960. The major studies of the embargo are Sears, *Jefferson and the Embargo*, and Walter W. Jennings, *The American Embargo, 1807-1809*, University of Iowa Studies in the Social Sciences, VIII, no 1 (Iowa City 1929).

47 TJ to Madison, 11 March 1808, *Works*, XI, 12-13, 15-17; to Levi Lincoln, 23 March 1808, *Writings*, XII, 21; to Bowdoin, 29 May 1808, *ibid.*, 69

48 TJ to Gallatin, 15 May 1808, *ibid.*, 56; to Gallatin, 6 May 1808, *ibid.*, 52-3; to General Benjamin Smith, 20 May 1808, *Works*, XI, 32; to Rush, 3 Jan. 1808, *Writings*, XI, 413

49 TJ, 'Eighth Annual Message,' 8 Nov. 1808, *Messages and Papers*, I, 440-1. Roger H. Brown, *The Republic in Peril: 1812* (New York 1964), 14, argues that Jefferson was determined to protect the republican experiment and that this necessarily entailed protecting American commerce.

50 TJ to Meriwether Lewis, 17 July 1808, *Works*, XI, 38-9; to Charles Pinckney, 30 March 1808, *Writings*, XII, 22-3; to William Lyman, 30 April 1808, *ibid.*, 42. For a theoretical discussion of the centralizing tendencies in war, see Stanislav Andreski, *Military Organization and Society* (Berkeley 1968), chap. V

51 Adams, *History*, II, iv, 277. Leonard Levy, *Jefferson and Civil Liberties: The Darker Side* (Cambridge, Mass. 1963), 93-4. For a discussion of the emotional appeals of war, see J. Glenn Gray, *The Warriors: Reflections on Men in Battle* (New York 1967), chap. ii; William James, 'The Moral Equivalent of War,' Leon Bramson and George W. Goethals, eds., *War: Studies from Psychology Sociology Anthropology* (New York 1968), 21-31

52 TJ to Monroe, 28 Jan. 1809, *Works*, XI, 96. See also to Mr Lieper, 25 May 1808, *Writings*, XII 65-6

53 TJ to de Nemours, 2 March 1809, Malone, *Correspondence*, 121; to General John Armstrong, 5 March 1809, *Writings*, XII, 261

54 TJ to Langdon, 2 Aug. 1808, *Works*, XI, 40; to Levi Lincoln, 13 Nov. 1808, *ibid.*, 74-5; Gallatin to TJ, 15 Nov. 1808, Adams, *Writings of Gallatin*, I, 399; TJ to Thomas Mann Randolph, 22 Nov. and 13 Dec. 1808, *Writings*, XVIII, 253, 257

55 Adams, *History*, II, iv, 165-6, 272-3; Sears, *Jefferson and the Embargo*, 4, 11, 30-1, 53, 74; Perkins, *Prologue to War*, 151-63; Levy, *Jefferson and Civil Liberties*, 95, 105-9;

M.D. Peterson, *Thomas Jefferson and the New Nation* (New York 1972), 885-6;
Malone, *Jefferson, 1805-1809*, 472-5, 483

56 Perkins, *Prologue to War*, 182. For the impact of the embargo, see *ibid.*, chap. v;
Sears, *Jefferson and the Embargo*, chaps. ix, x; Jennings, *American Embargo*, chaps. iv,
vi. Sears argues (pp. 319-20) that Jefferson's philosophy was vindicated, despite
the failure of his policy. Levy, *Jefferson and Civil Liberties*, 94-5, believes that
Jefferson failed dismally as a leader. Peterson and Malone find him wanting, but
not as badly as Levy. For a case study of the forces which led to the repeal of the
embargo, see John S. Pancake, 'Baltimore and the Embargo: 1808-1809,' *Maryland
Historical Magazine*, XLVII (1953), 173-87.

57 TJ to Thomas Mann Randolph, 2 Jan. 1809, *Writings*, XVIII, 257-9

58 TJ to Thomas Lieper, 21 Jan. 1809, *Works*, XI, 91; to Benjamin Stoddert, 18 Feb.
1809, *ibid.*, 98

CHAPTER 4: SAGE AND NATIONALIST

1 Homer cited in Gilbert Chinard, ed., *The Literary Bible of Thomas Jefferson: His
Commonplace Book of Philosophers and Poets* (Baltimore 1928), 110; TJ to Noah
Worcester, 26 Nov. 1817, Andrew A. Lipscomb and Albert Bergh, eds., *The
Writings of Thomas Jefferson* (Washington, DC 1903), XVIII, 298

2 R.J. Honeywell, 'President Jefferson and His Successor,' *American Historical Review*,
XLVI (1940), 64-75

3 TJ to Henry Dearborn, 16 July 1810, Paul Leicester Ford, ed., *The Works of Thomas
Jefferson* (New York 1905), XI, 144; to William Short, 8 March 1809, *ibid.*, 104; to
William Pinckney, 15 July 1810, *Writings*, XVIII, 265; S.D. Hoslett, 'Jefferson and
England: The Embargo as a Measure of Coercion,' *Americana*, XXXIV (1940), 53-4

4 TJ to Caesar A. Rodney, 10 Feb. 1810, *Works*, XI, 135; to Messrs Bloodgood and
Hammond, 30 Sept. 1809, *Writings*, XII, 317

5 TJ to John Monroe, 11 Dec. 1809, Missouri Historical Society, *Glimpses of the Past:
Correspondence of Thomas Jefferson, 1788-1826* (St Louis 1936), III, 112

6 TJ to James Madison, 17 March 1809, *Writings*, XII, 268; to William A. Burwell, 25
Feb. 1810, *ibid.*, 364

7 TJ to Madison, 27 and 17 April 1809, *ibid.*, 275, 305

8 TJ to Clement Caine, 16 Sept. 1811, *Works*, XI, 215-16; to Archibald Stuart, 11
Aug. and 14 Nov. 1811, *ibid.*, 210, 211; to Thomas Law, 15 Jan. 1811, *ibid.*, 164

9 On preparedness, see TJ to Thaddeus Kosciusko, 26 Feb. 1810, *Writings*, XII, 366-8;
to Dearborn, 14 Aug. 1811, *ibid.*, XIII, 73; on territorial expansion, see to John
Wayles Eppes, 5 Jan. 1811, *Works*, XI, 161; to Madison, 14 May 1820, *ibid.*, XII,
160-1; to John Armstrong, 5 March 1809, *Writings*, XII, 261; to Madison, 27 April
1809, *ibid.*, 276-7

10 TJ to Gallatin, 11 Oct. 1809, *Works*, XI, 125; to James Ogilvie, 4 Aug. 1811, *Writings*, XIII, 70

11 TJ to Madison, 24 April 1811, *Works*, XI, 203; to de Nemours, 15 April 1811, Dumas Malone, *Correspondence between Thomas Jefferson and Pierre Samuel DuPont de Nemours, 1798-1817*, trans. Linwood Lehman (Boston 1930), 132

12 TJ to Madison, 17 March 1809, *Writings*, XII, 267; to Caesar A. Rodney, *Works*, XI, 136; to Madison, 19 Feb. 1812, *ibid.*, 226

13 TJ to Charles Pinckney, 12 Feb. 1812, *Writings*, XVIII, 272. On 8 Jan. 1813 Jefferson wrote to Henry Middleton that 'nothing but the total prostration of all moral principle could have produced the enormities which have forced us at length into the war.' *Ibid.*, XIII, 202-3. For the right of a nation to use force, see to John B. Colvin, 20 Sept. 1810, *Works*, XI, 146-7; Gilbert Chinard, ed., *The Commonplace Book of Thomas Jefferson: A Repertory of His Ideas on Government* (Baltimore 1926), 99. On debt see to Eppes, 11 Sept. 1813, *Works*, XI, 308

14 TJ to Madison, 29 June 1812, *ibid.*, 262; to Adams, 11 June 1812, Lester J. Cappon, ed., *The Adams-Jefferson Letters* (Chapel Hill 1959), II, 308

15 TJ to George Logan, 13 Oct. 1813, *Works*, XI, 339; to Madame de Stael-Holstein, 24 May 1813, *Writings*, XIII, 241; to Short, 28 Nov. 1814, *ibid.*, XIV, 215-16

16 TJ to Madison, 30 May 1812, *Works*, XI, 247-8. Jefferson saw privateers as a militia of the oceans. See to Kosciusko, 26 June 1812, *ibid.*, 258-62; to Theodorus Bailey, 6 Feb. 1813, *Writings*, XIII, 217. For reference to a possible triangular war, see Leland R. Johnson, 'The Suspense Was Hell: The Senate Vote for War in 1812,' *Indiana Magazine of History*, LXV (1969), 247-67

17 TJ to Madison, 17 April 1812, *Works*, XI, 235; to James Ronaldson, 12 Jan. 1813, *ibid.*, 274

18 TJ to Short, 18 June 1813, *Writings*, XIII, 258; to Madison, 5 Aug. 1812, *ibid.*, 183

19 TJ to James Maury, 25 April 1812, *Works*, XI, 240; to Madame de Tesse, 8 Dec. 1813, *ibid.*, 361; to Robert Patterson, 11 Sept. 1811, *Writings*, XIII, 87

20 TJ to William Duane, 4 Aug. 1812, *Works*, XI, 265

21 TJ to Kosciusko, 28 June 1812, *ibid.*, 258-62; to Kosciusko, 5 Aug. 1812, *Writings*, XIII, 182-3; to Robert Wright, 8 Aug. 1812, *ibid.*, 184

22 TJ to William H. Crawford, 11 Feb. 1815, *Works*, XI, 450-1. For other examples of militancy, see to Philip Mazzei, 29 Dec. 1813, *ibid.*, 365; to Wright, 8 Aug. 1812, *Writings*, XIII, 184-5; to Thomas Letre, 8 Aug. 1812, *ibid.*, 185-6; to Stael-Holstein, 24 May 1813, *ibid.*, 241-3.

23 TJ to Madison, 6 Nov. 1812, *Works*, XI, 271; to Duane, 22 Jan. 1813, *Writings*, XIII, 215; to Bailey, 6 Feb. 1813, *ibid.*, 217; to Madison, 21 June 1813, *ibid.*, 265-8. Honeywell, 'Jefferson and Successor,' 74

24 TJ to von Humboldt, 6 Dec. 1813, *Works*, XI, 353-4; to Josiah Meigs, 18 Sept. 1813, *ibid.*, 335; to Kosciusko, 30 Nov. 1813, *Writings*, XIX, 204-5; to Thomas Cooper, 10

Sept. 1814, *ibid.*, XIV, 186. For a brief glimpse at the prisoner of war issue, see Ralph Robinson, 'Retaliation for the Treatment of Prisoners in the War of 1812,' *American Historical Review*, XLIV (1943), 65-70.

25 TJ as cited in M.D. Peterson, *Thomas Jefferson and the New Nation* (New York 1972), 933. See also to Short, 28 Nov. 1814, *Writings*, XIV, 214

26 TJ to Crawford, 11 Feb. 1815, *Works*, XI, 453-4; to Dearborn, 17 March 1815, *Writings*, XIV, 288; to Maury, 15 and 16 June 1815, *ibid.*, 311-12, 315-18; to Lafayette, 14 Feb. 1815, Gilbert Chinard, ed., *The Letters of Lafayette and Jefferson* (Baltimore 1929), 373

27 TJ to Adams, 5 July 1814, Cappon, *Adams-Jefferson Letters*, II, 431-2. On Napoleon as a counterbalance, see to John Clarke, 27 Jan. 1814, *Writings*, XIV, 80; L.S. Kaplan, 'Jefferson, the Napoleonic Wars, and the Balance of Power,' *William and Mary Quarterly*, 3d Series, XIV (1957), 196-217.

28 TJ to Adams, 10 June 1815, Cappon, *Adams-Jefferson Letters*, II, 442-3; to Lafayette, 17 May 1816, Chinard, *Letters of Lafayette and Jefferson*, 383

29 TJ to Thomas Leiper, 12 June 1815, *Works*, XI, 479; to Lafayette, 14 May 1817, Chinard, *Letters of Lafayette and Jefferson*, 389-90

30 TJ to Lafayette, 14 May 1817, *ibid.* Peterson, *Jefferson and New Nation*, 933-4, points out that the war brought personal financial hardship to Jefferson and believes that it shattered his optimism.

31 TJ to James Monroe, 4 Feb. 1817, *Works*, XI, 515-16; to Lafayette, 26 Dec. 1820, *ibid.*, XII, 191; to Dearborn, 5 July 1819, *Writings*, XIX, 272

32 TJ to Walter Jones, 5 March 1810, *Works*, XI, 139; to Caine, 16 Sept. 1811, *ibid.*, 214-15; to von Humboldt, 6 Dec. 1813, *ibid.*, 352

33 TJ to John Crawford, 2 Jan. 1812, *Writings*, XIII, 119. See also to Short, 4 Aug. 1820, *ibid.*, XV, 263; to Kosciusko, 13 April 1811, *ibid.*, XIII, 41-2

34 TJ to Madison, 23 March 1815, *Works*, XI, 466. See also to Leiper, 12 June 1815, *ibid.*, 477

35 TJ to Monroe, 11 June 1823, *ibid.*, XII, 292. See also to Adams, 1 June 1822, Cappon, *Adams-Jefferson Letters*, II, 578

36 TJ to Monroe, 24 Oct. 1823, *Works*, XII, 318-20. See T.R. Schellenberg, 'Jeffersonian Origins of the Monroe Doctrine,' *Hispanic American Historical Review*, XIV (1934), 1-31

37 TJ to William Wirt, 3 May 1811, *Works*, XI, 200. See also to Kosciusko, 13 April 1811, *Writings*, XIII, 41; to Thomas Cooper, 6 Aug. 1810, *ibid.*, XII, 403

38 TJ to Eppes, 11 Sept. 1813, *Works*, XI, 308; to Logan, 3 Oct. 1813, *ibid.*, 340-1; to Eppes, 9 Sept. 1814, *ibid.*, 426; to Madison, 15 Oct. 1814, *ibid.*, 432-5; to Monroe, 16 Oct. 1814, *ibid.*, 436-8. Sidney Forman, 'Thomas Jefferson on Universal Military Training,' *Military Affairs*, XI (1947), 177-8

39 TJ to David Bailey Warden, 26 Dec. 1820, *Works*, XII, 179

40 TJ to Short, 28 Nov. 1814, *Writings*, XIV, 213. See also to Adams, 1 June 1822, Cappon, *Adams-Jefferson Letters*, II, 578

41 TJ to Worcester, 29 Jan. 1816, *Writings*, XIV, 415-16; to Worcester, 26 Nov. 1817, *ibid.*, XVIII, 298-9. Jefferson had always been suspicious of Quaker pacifism because he believed it was rooted in loyalty to England. See to Samuel Kercheval, 19 Jan. 1810, *ibid.*, XII, 347

42 TJ to Cornelius Camden Blatchly, 21 Oct. 1822, *ibid.*, XV, 400; to William Ludlow, 6 Sept. 1824, *ibid.*, XVI, 74-5; to de Nemours, 24 April 1816, Malone, *Correspondence*, 186; to Adams, 16 April 1816 and 12 Sept. 1821, Cappon, *Adams-Jefferson Letters*, II, 467, 475

43 TJ to Say, 2 March 1815, *Writings*, XIV, 259-60. See also to James Jay, 7 April 1809, *ibid.*, XII, 271; to Cooper, 10 Sept. 1814, *ibid.*, XIV, 185; to William H. Crawford, 20 June 1816, *Works*, XI, 538-9. John U. Nef, *War and Human Progress* (New York 1963), 334-42

44 TJ to Adams, 1 Nov. 1822, Cappon, *Adams-Jefferson Letters*, II, 585

45 See for examples, TJ to Eppes, 24 June and 11 Sept. 1813, *Works*, XI, 298-304, 308-11; to Monroe, 1 Jan. 1815, *ibid.*, 443-4; to Madison, 15 Oct. 1814, *ibid.*, 432-5

46 TJ to A.C.V.C. Destutt de Tracy, 26 Dec. 1820, *ibid.*, XII, 184

47 TJ to Correa de Serra, 27 Dec. 1814, *Writings*, XIV, 222. Jefferson wanted Madison to publish a pamphlet on the War of 1812 to show, in part, that a certain amount of submission to wrong was wisdom and not pusillanimity. 23 March 1815, *Works*, XI, 464. See also to Adams, 1 June 1822, Cappon, *Adams-Jefferson Letters*, II, 579; Chinard, *Commonplace Book of Jefferson*, 369-72

48 Jomini, *The Art of War*, trans. G.H. Mendell and W.P. Craighill (Philadelphia 1862), 11-13, 23, 30-1. Crane Brinton *et al.*, 'Jomini,' in Edward Mead Earle, ed., *Makers of Modern Strategy: Military Thought from Machiavelli to Hitler* (Princeton 1941), 90-2

49 Excellent analyses of Clausewitz are Roger Ashley Leonard, ed., *A Short Guide to Clausewitz on War* (New York 1968), 3-37, and Hans Rothfels, 'Clausewitz,' in Earle, *Makers of Modern Strategy*, 93-113.

50 Burns, *The American Idea of Mission* (New Brunswick 1957), 257; see *ibid.*, chap. ix, 'War as an Instrument of National Mission.' For other essays on the American view of war, see Thomas A. Bailey, *The Man in the Street: The Impact of American Public Opinion on Foreign Policy* (New York 1948), chap. vii; Dexter Perkins, 'The American Attitude towards War,' *Yale Review*, XXXVIII (1948), 234-52; Robert E. Osgood, *Limited War: The Challenge to American Strategy* (Chicago 1957), chaps. i-ii.

51 Huntington, *The Soldier and the State: The Theory and Politics of Civil Military Relations* (Cambridge, Mass. 1957), 151; Kittredge, 'National Peace Objectives and War Aims from 1775-1955,' *Marine Corps Gazette*, XL (July 1956), 8-19

52 Shy, 'The American Military Experience: History and Learning,' *Journal of*

Interdisciplinary History, I (1971), 205-28; Russell F. Weigley, *The American Way of War* (New York 1973), xii-xiii, 18-19, 47; Bernard Brodie, *War and Politics* (New York 1973); Walter Millis, *Arms and Men* (New York 1956), 22-3, 58-65. See my own 'Thomas Jefferson and the Function of War: For Policy or Principle?' *Canadian Journal of History*, XI (1976), 154-71, and Charles A. Lofgren, 'Force and Diplomacy, 1846-1848: The View from Washington,' *Military Affairs*, XXXI (1967), 57-64.

Bibliography

The principal sources have been cited in the notes. This bibliography consists of works consulted which proved useful but did not always lend themselves to direct citation.

Students of Jefferson have been legion. Dumas Malone's *Jefferson and His Time* (Boston 1948-), 5 vols. to date, will be definitive when completed. Merrill D. Peterson's biography, *Thomas Jefferson and the New Nation* (New York 1972), is the best single-volume work, and in *The Jeffersonian Image in the American Mind* (New York 1960), Peterson traces how succeeding generations of Americans have viewed Jefferson. Fawn M. Brodie, *Thomas Jefferson: An Intimate History* (New York 1974), is an attempt at psychological analysis. See also Joseph Dorfman, 'The Economic Philosophy of Thomas Jefferson,' *Political Science Quarterly*, LV (1940), 98-121; Robert E. Shalhope, 'Thomas Jefferson's Republicanism and Antebellum Southern Thought,' *Journal of Southern History*, XLII (1976), 529-56. Jefferson is seen as a pacifist in Edwin D. Mead, 'Washington, Jefferson, and Franklin on War,' *World Peace Foundation Pamphlet*, Series no 5, III (1919), and in Louis M. Sears. 'Jefferson and the Law of Nations,' *American Political Science Review*, XIII (1919), 379-99. For monographs on Jefferson's foreign policy, see William Kirk Woolery, *The Relation of Thomas Jefferson to American Foreign Policy, 1783-1793* (Baltimore 1927); John Latane Halladay, 'Jefferson's Influence on American Foreign Policy,' University of Virginia, *Alumni Bulletin*, 3d Series, XVII (1924), 245-69; Lawrence S. Kaplan, 'Jefferson's Foreign Policy and Napoleon's Ideologues,' *William and Mary Quarterly*, 3d Series, XIX (1962), 344-59, and 'The Consensus of 1789: Jefferson and Hamilton on American Foreign Policy,' *South Atlantic Quarterly*, LXXI (1972), 91-105; A.H. Bowman, 'Jefferson, Hamilton, and American Foreign Policy,' *Political Science Quarterly*, LXXI (1956), 18-41; J.W. Bradley, 'W.C.C. Claiborne and Spain: Foreign Affairs under Jefferson and Madison, 1801-1811,' *Louisiana History*, XII (1971), 297-314, and XIII (1972), 5-26; Reginald C. Stuart, 'Thomas Jefferson and the Function of War: Policy or Principle?' *Canadian Journal of History*, XI (1976), 154-71; David Lindsey, 'George Canning and Jefferson's Embargo, 1807-1809,' *Tyler's*

Quarterly, I (1952), 43-7. Jefferson's intellectual background is evident in E. Millicent Sowerby, comp., *The Catalogue of the Library of Thomas Jefferson* (Washington, DC 1952), 5 vols., and H.T. Colbourn, 'Thomas Jefferson's Use of the Past,' *William and Mary Quarterly*, 3d Series, XV (1958), 57-70.

There is no satisfactory study of war in the eighteenth century. The works by John U. Nef, *War and Human Progress: An Essay on the Rise of Industrial Civilization* (New York 1963), and Elizabeth V. Souleyman, *The Vision of World Peace in Seventeenth and Eighteenth-Century France* (New York 1941), are the most comprehensive. The best general studies of war remain Quincy Wright, *A Study of War* (Chicago 1942), 2 vols., and Theodore Ropp, *War in the Modern World* (New York 1962). A brief survey by an expert is Michael Howard, *War in European History* (London 1976). See also Fritz Grob, *The Relativity of War and Peace: A Study in Law, History, and Politics* (New Haven 1949); Hans Speier, 'Militarism in the Eighteenth Century,' in Speier, *Social Order and the Risks of War* (Cambridge, Mass. 1969), 230-52; Henry Guerlac, 'Vauban: The Impact of Science on War,' in Edward Mead Earle, ed., *Makers of Modern Strategy: Military Thought from Machiavelli to Hitler* (Princeton 1941), 26-48; R.R. Palmer, 'Frederick the Great, Guibert, Bülow: From Dynastic to National War,' in *ibid.*, 49-74. Sir George N. Clark, *War and Society in the Seventeenth Century* (Cambridge 1958), is applicable to the mid-eighteenth century. Insight into the limited-war mentality may be gained from reading Count Saxe, *Reveries or Memoirs upon the Art of War* (Westport, Conn. 1971); Edwin Canaan, ed., *Lectures on Justice, Police, Revenue and Arms Delivered in the University of Glasgow by Adam Smith*, reported by a student in 1763 (Oxford 1896), 267-74; and the commentary and documents in Geoffrey Symcox, ed., *War, Diplomacy and Imperialism, 1618-1763* (New York 1973).

The views of the churches may be found in Roland Bainton, *Christian Attitudes toward War and Peace* (New York 1960); Michael Walzer, *Revolution of the Saints: A Study in the Origins of Radical Politics* (Cambridge, Mass. 1965), chap. viii; T.S.K. Scott-Craig, *Christian Attitudes to War and Peace: A Study of the Four Main Types* (New York 1938); James T. Johnson, *Ideology, Reason, and the Limitation of War: Religious and Secular Concepts, 1200-1740* (Princeton 1975); Bainton, 'Congregationalism: From the Just War to the Crusade in the Puritan Revolution,' Andover Newton Theological School, *Bulletin*, XXXV (1943), 1-20; Arthur H. Buffinton, 'The Puritan View of War,' Colonial Society of Massachusetts, *Publications*, XXVIII (1930-3), 69-86; and Jon A.T. Alexander, 'Colonial New England Preaching on War as Illustrated in Massachusetts Artillery Election Sermons,' *Journal of Church and State*, XVII (1975), 423-42.

Theory and practice in international law are well treated by Arthur Nussbaum, *A Concise History of the Law of Nations* (New York 1954), 17-114. This should be supplemented by F.H. Hinsley, *Power and the Pursuit of Peace: Theory and Practice in the History of Relations between States* (Cambridge 1967); Carl J. Friedrich, *Inevitable Peace* (Cambridge, Mass. 1948), which concentrates on Immanuel Kant; Sidney Bailey, *Prohibitions and Restraints in War* (London 1972); the introduction and documents in Symcox, *War, Diplomacy, and Imperialism*; M. Bernard, 'The Growth of Laws and Usages of War,' *Oxford Essays*, II (1856); and Richard Shelly Hartigan, 'Noncombatant Immunity: Reflections on Its Origin and Present Status,' *Review of Politics*, XXIX (1967), 204-20. For the diplomacy of the age, see Felix Gilbert, *To the Farewell Address: Ideas of Early American Foreign Policy* (Princeton 1961); and Albert Sorel, *Europe under the Old Regime*, trans. Francis Herrich (New York 1964). For the works of the legists, the best to study is Hugo Grotius, *The Rights of War and Peace*, trans. A.C. Campbell (New York 1911), but also see Samuel Pufendorf, *De Officio Hominis et Civis Juxta Legem Naturalem Libri Duo*, trans. Frank Gardner Moore (New York 1927); and Cornelius Van Bynkershoek, *Quaestionum Juris Publici Libri Duo*, trans. Tenny Frank (Oxford 1930). Sections of Thomas Hobbes, *Leviathan: Or, Matter, Form, and Power of a Commonwealth Ecclesiastical and Civil* (Chicago 1952); John Locke, *Two Treatises of Government*, ed. Peter Laslett (Cambridge 1960), along with Richard Cox, *Locke on War and Peace* (Oxford 1960); William Blackstone, *Commentaries on the Laws of England: Of Public Wrongs* (Boston 1962), IV; and Charles de Secondat, Baron de Montesquieu, *The Spirit of Laws*, trans. Thomas Nugent (Chicago 1952), are all pertinent to an understanding of the eighteenth-century view of war.

An indication of how whig and republican ideas wafted across the Atlantic and permeated American thinking can be found in Benjamin Wright, *American Interpretations of Natural Law: A Study in the Historical Process of Political Thought* (Cambridge, Mass. 1931); Charles Mullett, *Fundamental Law and the American Revolution, 1760-1776* (New York 1933); Bernard Bailyn, *The Ideological Origins of the American Revolution* (Cambridge, Mass. 1967); H. Trevour Colbourn, *The Lamp of Experience* (Chapel Hill 1965), Ronald E. Pynn, 'The Influence of John Locke's Political Philosophy on the American Revolution,' *North Dakota Quarterly*, XIII (1974), 48-56; Clinton Rossiter, *The Seedtime of the Republic* (New York 1953); and Henry F. May, *The Enlightenment in America* (New York 1976).

Peter Brock has given modern pacifism encyclopaedic treatment in *Pacifism in Europe to 1914* (Princeton 1972), and *Pacifism in the United States: From the Colonial Era to the First World War* (Princeton 1968). Merle Curti, *The American Peace Crusade, 1815-1860* (Durham 1929), and *Peace or War: The American Struggle, 1636-1936* (New York 1936), can still be read with profit. See also Souleyman, *Vision of World Peace*; Carl J. Friedrich, *Inevitable Peace* (Cambridge, Mass. 1948); Sylvester John Hemleben, *Plans for World Peace through Six Centuries* (New York 1972); Robert D.W. Connor, 'Josiah Tucker or Cassandra Picks the Pocket of Mars,' *World Politics*, CIII (1940), 79-90; and Stanley Hoffmann, *The State of War: Essays on the Theory and Practice of International Politics* (New York 1965), 54-87, for an essay on Jean-Jacques Rousseau. Roger E. Sappington, 'North Carolina and the Non-Resistant Sects during the American War of Independence,' *Quaker History*, LX (1971), 29-47, offers a case study of American pacifism in a war setting.

Works on military history were only occasionally useful for this study. Marcus Cunliffe, *Soldiers and Civilians: The Martial Spirit in America, 1775-1865* (Boston 1968), is the best on the subject, although Arthur A. Ekirch, *The Civilian and the Military* (New York 1956), is more chronologically extensive. For attitudes towards the navy, see Marshall Smelser, *The Congress Founds the Navy, 1787-1798* (Notre Dame 1959). The treatment of prisoners during the American wars of Jefferson's time has received surprisingly wide study. See William Dabney, *After Saratoga: The Story of the Convention Army* (Albuquerque 1954); John K. Alexander, 'American Privateersmen in the Mill Prison during 1777-1782: An Evaluation,' Essex Institute, *Historical Collections*, CII (1966), 318-40, and 'Forton Prison during the American Revolution: A Case Study of British Prisoner of War Policy and the American Prisoner Response to that Policy,' *ibid.*, CIII (1967), 365-89; Richard H. Amerman, 'Treatment of American Prisoners during the Revolution,' New Jersey Historical Society, *Proceedings*, LXXVIII (1960), 257-75; Olive Anderson, 'The Treatment of Prisoners of War in Britain during the American War of Independence,' Institute of Historical Research, *Bulletin*, XXVIII (1955), 68-83; David Savageau, 'The United States Navy and Its "Half War" Prisoners, 1798-1801,' *American Neptune*, XXXI (1971), 159-76; and Ralph Robinson, 'Retaliation for the Treatment of Prisoners in the War of 1812,' *American Historical Review*, XLIX (1943), 65-70.

The diplomatic history of Jefferson's time is rich with fine studies. Old, but still informative, are the essays in Samuel Flagg Bemis, ed., *The American Secretaries of State and Their Diplomacy* (New York 1927), vols. I-IV. Paul A. Varg, *Foreign Policies of the Founding Fathers* ([East Lansing] 1963); Doris A. Graber, *Public Opinion, the President, and Foreign Policy: Four Case Studies from the Formative Years* (New York 1968); and Lawrence S. Kaplan, *Colonies into Nation: American Diplomacy, 1763-1801* (New York 1972), all provide broad surveys. Ray Irwin covers *The Diplomatic Relations of the United States with the Barbary Powers, 1776-1816* (Chapel Hill 1931), the best, despite more recent popular accounts. J. Fred Rippy and Angie Debo, *The Historical Background of the American Policy of Isolation* (Northampton 1924), and Louis B. Wright, 'The Founding Fathers and "Splendid Isolation," ' *Huntington Library Quarterly*, VI (1943), 173-96, give depth to the issue of isolation, and John A. Logan, *No Transfer: An American Security Principle* (New Haven 1961), works out its ramifications.

For the Revolution and Confederation periods, Richard B. Morris, *The Peacemakers: The Great Powers and American Independence* (New York 1965), is the best work on that subject. Frederick W. Marks, III, *Independence on Trial: Foreign Affairs and the Making of the Constitution* (Baton Rouge 1973), partly fills a long-standing gap in the literature. The standard work on the southwest is Arthur P. Whitaker, *The Spanish-American Frontier,*

1783-1795 (New York 1927), although Alexander DeConde, *This Affair of Louisiana* (New York 1976), is an up-to-date synthesis. See Bernard Donahoe and Marshall Smelser, 'The Congressional Power to Raise Armies: The Constitutional and Ratifying Conventions, 1787-1788,' *Review of Politics*, XXX (1971), 202-11, and James A. Carr, 'John Adams and the Barbary Problem: The Myth and the Record,' *American Neptune*, XXVI (1966), 229-57, for other helpful studies.

Washington's presidencies have received much attention. See especially Alexander DeConde, *Entangling Alliances: Politics and Diplomacy under George Washington* (Durham 1958); Charles S. Hyneman, *The First American Neutrality* (Urbana 1934); Gerald A. Combs, *The Jay Treaty: Political Battleground of the Founding Fathers* (Berkeley 1970); Harry Ammon, *The Genet Mission* (New York 1973); Charles M. Thomas, *American Neutrality in 1793: A Study in Cabinet Government* (New York 1931); and Samuel Flagg Bemis, *Jay's Treaty: A Study in Commerce and Diplomacy* (New York 1923), 'The Background of Washington's Foreign Policy,' *Yale Review*, XVI (1927), 316-36, and 'The United States and the Abortive Armed Neutrality of 1794,' *American Historical Review*, XXIV (1918), 26-47.

Adams' presidency and the Quasi-War have received good treatment from varying perspectives. A well-rounded view can be obtained by reading Manning Dauer, *The Adams Federalists* (Baltimore 1953); Stephen G. Kurtz, *The Presidency of John Adams: The Collapse of Federalism, 1795-1800* (Philadelphia 1957); Gerard H. Clarfield, *Timothy Pickering and American Diplomacy, 1795-1800* (Columbia, Missouri 1969); Alexander DeConde, *The Quasi-War: The Politics and Diplomacy of the Undeclared War with France, 1797-1801* (New York 1966); Peter P. Hill, *William Vans Murray Federalist Diplomat: The Shaping of the Peace with France, 1797-1801* (Syracuse 1971); Bradford Perkins, *The First Rapprochement: England and the United States, 1795-1805* (Philadelphia 1955); E. Wilson Lyon, 'The Directory and the United States,' *American Historical Review*, XLIII (1938), 514-32; Frederick B. Tolles, 'Unofficial Ambassador: George Logan's Mission to France, 1798,' *William and Mary Quarterly*, 3d Series, VII (1950), 3-25; and William G. Anderson, 'John Adams, the Navy and the Quasi-War with France,' *American Neptune*, XXX (1970), 117-32. For military affairs, see the excellent book by Richard Kohn, *Eagle and Sword: The Beginnings of the Military Establishment in America* (New York 1975), and William Gaines, Jr., 'The Forgotten Army: Recruiting for a National Emergency (1799-1800),' *Virginia Magazine of History and Biography*, LVI (1948), 267-79. The documents in James B. Scott, ed., *The Controversy over Neutral Rights between the United States and France, 1797-1800: A Collection of American State Papers and Judicial Decisions* (New York 1917), provide a legal perspective on the limited war with France.

Jefferson's presidencies are best studied through the works of Malone and Peterson, as well as those cited in the notes for Chapter 3. A new synthesis is Forrest McDonald, *The Presidency of Thomas Jefferson* (Lawrence, Kansas 1976). An ideological perspective in keeping with the recent historiographical emphasis on republicanism is Roger H.

Brown, *The Republic in Peril: 1812* (New York 1964). William Gribbin, *The Churches Militant: The War of 1812 and American Religion* (New Haven 1973), studies the interrelationship of the war and religious thought. Bradford Perkins, *Prologue to War: England and the United States, 1805-1812* (Berkeley 1961), is the best work to read for the diplomacy leading up to the War of 1812. Journal articles provide valuable perspective, however, and readers should consult Lawrence Kaplan, 'France and Madison's Decision for War, 1812,' *Mississippi Valley Historical Review*, L (1964), 652-71, and 'France and the War of 1812,' *Journal of American History*, LVII (1970), 36-47; and Norman K. Risjord, '1812: Conservatives, War Hawks, and the Nation's Honor,' *William and Mary Quarterly*, 3d Series, XVIII (1961), 196-211. Federalist separatism is studied in J.S. Martel, 'A Side Light on Federalist Strategy during the War of 1812,' *American Historical Review*, XLIII (1938), 553-66. See also Theodore Clarke Smith, 'War Guilt in 1812,' Massachusetts Historical Society, *Proceedings*, LXIV (1931), 319-45.

The significance of republican ideology for the period of Jefferson's life is apparent in two works: Gordon S. Wood, *The Creation of the American Republic, 1776-1787* (Chapel Hill 1969), and Richard Buel, Jr., *Securing the Revolution: Ideology in American Politics, 1789-1815* (Ithaca 1972). For the significance of this theme, see Robert E. Shalhope, 'Toward a Republican Synthesis: The Emergence of an Understanding of Republicanism in American Historiography,' *William and Mary Quarterly*, 3d Series, XXIX (1972), 49-80.

The diplomacy of the period between the War of 1812 and Jefferson's death can be followed in the essays in Samuel Flagg Bemis, ed., *The American Secretaries of State and Their Diplomacy* (New York 1927); Bradford Perkins, *Castlereagh and Adams: England and the United States, 1812-1823* (Berkeley 1964); and Bemis, *John Quincy Adams and the Foundations of American Diplomacy* (New York 1949). Ernest R. May, *The Making of the Monroe Doctrine* (Cambridge, Mass. 1975), attempts a domestic political interpretation, reducing the significance of ideology.

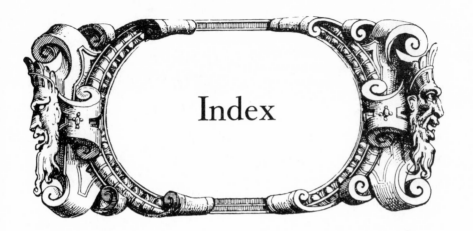

Index

List 10.00